# Entertaining Your Indoor Cat

# Entertaining Your Indoor Cat

## 50 Fun and Inventive Amusements for Your Indoor Cat

**KEVIN P. KELLY**

Illustrations by Wendy Crowell

SELLERS

PUBLISHING

Published by
**Sellers Publishing, Inc.**

161 John Roberts Road, South Portland, Maine 04106
For ordering information:
(800) 625-3386 toll-free
(207) 772-6814 fax

Illustrations: Wendy Crowell
Design: Heather Zschock

ISBN 13: 978-1-4162-0517-3

Printed in the U.S.A.

# Dedication

To all the top cats, hep cats, and cool cats I've had the
pleasure of knowing and entertaining, especially Juan,
Forrest, Pie, Mama, Baby J., and Marble.

Thanks for allowing me, a mere human, to experience
a bit of your fabulous feline world and for indulging my
obsessive need to rub your heads, open and close doors
for you, and obey your daily commands.

# Contents

Acknowledgments . . . . . . . . . . . . . . . . . . . . . . . . . . . . . . . . . . . . . . . 9

Introduction . . . . . . . . . . . . . . . . . . . . . . . . . . . . . . . . . . . . . . . . . . 10

## Part One: Entertaining Kittens

### DANGLING STRINGS & RIBBONS

The Lazy String . . . . . . . . . . . . . . . . . . . . . . . . . . . . . . . . . . . 15

The Hypnotic Belly Tickle . . . . . . . . . . . . . . . . . . . . . . . . . . 16

Flick 'n' Fly . . . . . . . . . . . . . . . . . . . . . . . . . . . . . . . . . . . . . . . 17

Pole Fishin' . . . . . . . . . . . . . . . . . . . . . . . . . . . . . . . . . . . . . . . 18

Bucket Fly . . . . . . . . . . . . . . . . . . . . . . . . . . . . . . . . . . . . . . . . . 20

Wiggly Ribbon Snake . . . . . . . . . . . . . . . . . . . . . . . . . . . . . . . 21

### STUFF ON A STRING

Yo-Yo Mouse . . . . . . . . . . . . . . . . . . . . . . . . . . . . . . . . . . . . . . 23

Rodeo Mouse and Cowboy Kitten . . . . . . . . . . . . . . . . . . . 24

Catnip Pull . . . . . . . . . . . . . . . . . . . . . . . . . . . . . . . . . . . . . . . . 26

### FASCINATION GAMES

Gone Fishin' . . . . . . . . . . . . . . . . . . . . . . . . . . . . . . . . . . . . . . 29

Pinwheel on a Stick . . . . . . . . . . . . . . . . . . . . . . . . . . . . . . . . 31

I'm Forever Chasing Bubbles . . . . . . . . . . . . . . . . . . . . . . . . 32

Birdies Through a Window . . . . . . . . . . . . . . . . . . . . . . . . . . 34

Squirrel Surprise . . . . . . . . . . . . . . . . . . . . . . . . . . . . . . . . . . . 36

### HOLD ON & NEVER LET GO!

Rassle the Tassel . . . . . . . . . . . . . . . . . . . . . . . . . . . . . . . . . . . 38

Clutch and Kill (not really!) . . . . . . . . . . . . . . . . . . . . . . . . . 40

Kitten Caboose . . . . . . . . . . . . . . . . . . . . . . . . . . . . . . . . . . . . 42

# Part Two: Adult Entertainment

## WORKOUT GAMES

Flashlight Romp . . . . . . . . . . . . . . . . . . . . . . . . . . . . . . . . . . . . . . 47

Crazy Susan . . . . . . . . . . . . . . . . . . . . . . . . . . . . . . . . . . . . . . . . . 48

Teeter-Totter Tumble . . . . . . . . . . . . . . . . . . . . . . . . . . . . . . . . . 50

Mouse Toss! . . . . . . . . . . . . . . . . . . . . . . . . . . . . . . . . . . . . . . . . . 51

Ping-Pong Paws . . . . . . . . . . . . . . . . . . . . . . . . . . . . . . . . . . . . . . 52

Ice Cube Hockey . . . . . . . . . . . . . . . . . . . . . . . . . . . . . . . . . . . . . 54

Roller Can Derby . . . . . . . . . . . . . . . . . . . . . . . . . . . . . . . . . . . . . 56

## TECHNO GAMES

Motor Mouse and His Robot Friends . . . . . . . . . . . . . . . . . . . . . 59

Screen Savior . . . . . . . . . . . . . . . . . . . . . . . . . . . . . . . . . . . . . . . . 64

Laser Sprite! . . . . . . . . . . . . . . . . . . . . . . . . . . . . . . . . . . . . . . . . . 66

Saturday Matinee . . . . . . . . . . . . . . . . . . . . . . . . . . . . . . . . . . . . . 68

Tunes for Cats to Groove on . . . . . . . . . . . . . . . . . . . . . . . . . . . 70

## BELLY UP!

Leather Glove Tickle . . . . . . . . . . . . . . . . . . . . . . . . . . . . . . . . . . 73

Flying Feathers . . . . . . . . . . . . . . . . . . . . . . . . . . . . . . . . . . . . . . . 74

The Elusive Peacock Feather . . . . . . . . . . . . . . . . . . . . . . . . . . . . 75

MouseStickle . . . . . . . . . . . . . . . . . . . . . . . . . . . . . . . . . . . . . . . . . 76

## BATTER UP!

Toss 'n' Swat . . . . . . . . . . . . . . . . . . . . . . . . . . . . . . . . . . . . . . . . 78

Pitch 'n' Catch . . . . . . . . . . . . . . . . . . . . . . . . . . . . . . . . . . . . . . . 79

Paper Ball Pop-ups . . . . . . . . . . . . . . . . . . . . . . . . . . . . . . . . . . . 80

Volleyball Smackdown! . . . . . . . . . . . . . . . . . . . . . . . . . . . . . . . . 81

## THE GREAT INDOORS

African Safari Theme Park . . . . . . . . . . . . . . . . . . . . . . . . . . . . . . . . . .84

Pussy's Playground . . . . . . . . . . . . . . . . . . . . . . . . . . . . . . . . . . . . . . . . .86

## THE GREAT (SAFE) OUTDOORS

Kitty Escapade with Harness and Leash . . . . . . . . . . . . . . . . . . . . . .89

Double Cat Fantasy . . . . . . . . . . . . . . . . . . . . . . . . . . . . . . . . . . . . . . . .94

Stakeout . . . . . . . . . . . . . . . . . . . . . . . . . . . . . . . . . . . . . . . . . . . . . . . . .96

# Part Three: Projects to Assemble

Stairway to the Stars . . . . . . . . . . . . . . . . . . . . . . . . . . . . . . . . . . . . .102

The Leaning Tower of Kitties . . . . . . . . . . . . . . . . . . . . . . . . . . . . . .106

Outdoor Enclosures . . . . . . . . . . . . . . . . . . . . . . . . . . . . . . . . . . . . . .108

Tunnel of Love . . . . . . . . . . . . . . . . . . . . . . . . . . . . . . . . . . . . . . . . . .110

Crinkle, Crinkle, Little Cat . . . . . . . . . . . . . . . . . . . . . . . . . . . . . . . .114

The Mr. Kitty Portable Self-Grooming Device . . . . . . . . . . . . . . . .118

# Part Four: Chillin' Out

Kitty Kneads Me . . . . . . . . . . . . . . . . . . . . . . . . . . . . . . . . . . . . . . . . .124

Cats-on-tumtum-asana . . . . . . . . . . . . . . . . . . . . . . . . . . . . . . . . . . . .126

# Acknowledgments

Many thanks and a big flick of the tail to Robin Haywood, publishing director extraordinaire; Diana, Tim, and Lucy Kipp for a great idea and inspiration; Wendy Crowell for her sweet, delightful art; Darren Defoe for more wacky ideas than most cats have; and Forrest and Pie for agreeing to test out all of the games in advance and assign them a suitable rating.

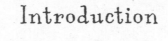

# Introduction

**When was the last time your cat read a good book?** Played
a round of golf? Or ordered the latest new release from
Netflix? Well, if your cat is like mine, the answer, of course,
is "never". As clever, resourceful, and wise as most cats
are, they don't enjoy the same kinds of leisure activities we
humans do. Cats perceive, take pleasure in, and interact
with the world in ways we can't imagine. However, they do
love to play, just as we do, and they most certainly enjoy
entertainment. And if a cat is an indoor cat, which is the best
lifestyle choice to ensure a cat's health and longevity, she is
especially dependent on her humans for play and interesting
diversions. *Entertaining Your Indoor Cat* will provide readers
with a variety of easy, innovative, and fun games and activities
designed to keep their indoor cats active, engaged, and happy.

I've been playing with and entertaining my own cats for
many years, and along the way, I've discovered, adapted, and
invented a vast array of simple, low-maintenance strategies
to keep my cats content and energetic. Although some cat
parents may believe that their lethargic fat cat is enjoying life,
snoozing on the couch or dozing on the windowsill, the truth
is that cats need to play and socialize. While they can make
do dreaming away most of their day, fun and intriguing

activities should be a part of every cat's life. Playtime for a cat is essential.

*Entertaining Your Indoor Cat,* with illustrations by Wendy Crowell, contains 50 games, activities, and simple projects that cat parents will have fun trying and adapting, and are designed to help feline friendly humans entertain, stimulate, and interact with their kitty pals. The book is divided into four sections: "Entertaining Kittens" (gentle fun for baby cats), "Adult Entertainment" (more vigorous activities), "Projects to Assemble" (simple do-it-yourself constructions), and "Just Chillin'" (relaxing ways to wind down with your cat). Useful, engaging resources — from kitty Web sites to cat magazines and organizations — are included throughout the book and are all devoted to cats and the people in their lives who are eager to be active participants in their kitties' health and well-being.

*Entertaining Your Indoor Cat* is a funny, interactive, all-inclusive guide for loving, concerned, and even exasperated cat people who want to keep their kitties at the top of their game. This book shows humans how to interact with their cats in ways that will amuse and entertain themselves as well as their feline friends.

Kevin Kelly

# PART ONE:

# Entertaining Kittens

Kittens start actively playing when they are around three to four weeks old. At that age the adorable puff balls begin to try out their stalking skills, pouncing and grabbing items and delivering little death blow kicks with their back paws. These playful moves may actually be hunting techniques they're instinctively developing at an early age. Of course, they may also just be fooling around and burning up all that kitten energy, like any toddler, riding in circles in the backyard on a clattering plastic Big Wheels. Whatever the reason, once kittens reach that certain age, they need and enjoy playtime with other kittens and with their human companions.

The following games for kittens are gentle fun for your baby mouser who's just beginning to learn the ropes and is starting to flex his claws and muscles.

Later in this section and in "Adult Entertainment" you'll discover all sorts of rough 'n' tumble, dynamic activities your older kittens and adult cats will enjoy. For now, if you have very young kittens, your best bet is to keep things simple. Let them gently discover the world of play as they learn how much fun they can have interacting with their human companions.

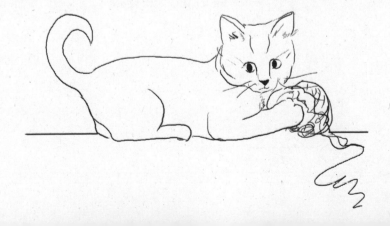

# DANGLING STRINGS & RIBBONS

Kittens, like all toddlers, are delighted by and curious about all sorts of ordinary things. Often the simplest items provide them with the greatest entertainment. Strings and ribbons may not be a big deal to the jaded adult population of cats or humans, but to kittens these tempting bits of floating cord and colorful satin can make an ordinary day exciting. With a little imagination, which kittens have in abundance, these simple activities provide moments of giddy fun that will brighten any kitty's day.

**CAUTION:** Small bits of ribbon or string can be hazardous to a cat or kitten's health. Be careful not to let these items shred or break unless you're prepared to dispose of them right away. Cats and kittens shouldn't be allowed to swallow this type of material, but given the opportunity they may do so.

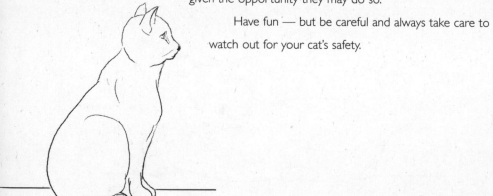

Have fun — but be careful and always take care to watch out for your cat's safety.

# The Lazy String

Here's the perfect game to help develop your kitten's paw-eye coordination. It doesn't take much effort on your part, and it serves as a gentle introduction to the fine art of swatting. It's a simple game, but remember that this is all new to her, and discovery is part of the fun.

## What You'll Need

- A piece of string three or four feet long (thicker string tends to sway better)
- A comfortable chair to sit in
- Room to roam — a space big enough to drag the string around so the kitten' can follow

## How It Works

Wave a long piece of thick string in front of your curious kitten. Gently sway the string back and forth like a pendulum in front of kitty. She'll try to grab it and will probably miss, but let her keep trying. She's still just a toddler, after all, who's learning the ropes — or strings, in this case. Eventually, she'll pick up the rhythm and start connecting with the string.

Once you have the kitten's attention, let her follow the string as you drag it across the floor, up and over objects, or through a kitty tunnel.

You'll probably grow tired of The Lazy String before your kitten does. If so, hand off the string to a human teammate who's willing to keep the game going.

# The Hypnotic Belly Tickle

If your kitten is like most baby cats, she'll lose her balance on a fairly regular basis. If this happens while she's playing the Lazy String, consider this Belly Tickle variation.

## What You'll Need

• The same equipment needed for the Lazy String: string, a chair, and your kitten

## How It Works

Allow the Lazy String to flow gently across the kitten's plump little gut. Let it drift along her face and neck, then down along her body. She'll be wiggling on her back, pawing at the string, and trying out her back leg pump. Chances are she'll never actually grab the string, but it's a lot of fun watching her try.

Some kittens tend to get a bit mesmerized by the Lazy String, whether they are lying on their backs or sitting or standing. If this happens, keep the string going. It doesn't mean your kitty's lost interest, she's just being a cat. After all, these are the same creatures who can sit for hours, staring at a hole, waiting for a (perhaps imaginary) mouse to appear.

# Flick 'n' Fly

If you enjoy fly fishing, you'll like this game, but most humans and their kitten pals have fun with Flick 'n' Fly whether they're fisher-folks or not. Play this one, and you'll develop a bit of the angler's skill yourself trying to land your kitten.

## What You'll Need

- A suitable length of string, about two to three feet long (The flicking action is harder to manage with longer pieces.)
- Optional: fly, bait toy, or treat. Lightweight, plastic novelty bugs work well and give kitty something to aim for. Keep them small for kitten-size fun, and she won't be intimidated.

## How It Works

Trot out your trusty string — this time with a little attachment. Tie a triple-knot on the end of the string to give it a bit of weight. You can attach a small toy, such as a plastic bug, or even a treat (a large, soft Pounce) to the end, but a knot works even better. This weight will serve as your fly when you're out fishing for kittens.

Next, flick your string/knot combo toward kitty and see if she takes the bait. See how close you can land the knot to her paw or some other suitable target, then pull it away across the floor and watch her chase it.

Scoring? Why not? But Flick 'n' Fly really is a win-win activity. Score one for you if kitty takes the bait — and one for her, too. She wants to catch the lure as much as you want to haul in the kitty.

# Pole Fishin'

A variation of Flick 'n' Fly, this game requires a higher skill level — you have to master the art of fly flicking while using a pole. But this can be a fun challenge for you and an entertaining interlude for your kitten.

## What You'll Need

- A thin garden stake or plastic kitty toy wand
- A suitable length of flickable string
- A small plastic bug or toy

## How It Works

As in traditional Flick 'n' Fly, you'll enjoy mastering the art of the flick; however, your wrist action here is closer to the traditional fly-fishing technique you've, perhaps, always dreamed about perfecting. Now the pole has become an extension of your wrist — you will become one with the knot or plastic bug at the end of the line — a Zen master of kitty fishing.

So, maybe you're not decked out in hip waders, battling a trophy trout in the middle of the Yellowstone River. Your kitten will still be mighty impressed by Mom's or Dad's fishing prowess.

The object of the game remains the same: Land the bait near the target zone and watch your kitten grab it.

After securing your string to the end of the pole, start casting your fly around your kitten. Try landing the fly near various toys, under a chair, or on a table. Drag the fly across the floor and let kitty race after it. Wherever it lands, she'll be eager to chase it.

# Bucket Fly

This variation of Pole Fishin' gives you (or the wannabe angler in your home) a real target to aim at, and it keeps your kitten intrigued while presenting her with another challenge: nabbing the pesky fly that's disappeared into the bucket.

## What You'll Need

- A bucket, box, or basket
- Your trusty fly flickin' pole and string
- A small plastic bug or toy for your fly

## How It Works

Master your flicking technique even more by aiming at the bucket. The object is to get your fly — whether it's a knot, a plastic bug, or a treat — to land in the container.

Place your bucket or other suitable container on the floor and show it to your kitten. As in the other Fly Flicking games, begin casting your line around kitty. This time, though, play keep-away, and gradually move the fly away from the curious cat and closer to the container. Next, try to land the fly inside the bucket — if you do, score one for you!

Your kitten will be watching the fly sail through the air, and she'll want to go after it when you've scored and landed the fly in the bucket. But don't be surprised if kitty leaps in the air to catch the fly before it lands in the bucket.

Chasing and catching the fly will be all the more challenging and inviting if "Baby Claws" has to hunt for it and scoop it out of a fascinating container.

# Wiggly Ribbon Snake

Here's a game that's convenient to play when you're wrapping presents. Take a break from tangling with all those Happy Birthday gift wrapping sheets and give the gift of fun to your kitten.

## What You'll Need

- A roll of gift-wrapping ribbon, one inch wide
- A room with enough floor space to roll out your ribbon

## How It Works

If you've been buried in paper, wrapping gifts, chances are you've already captured your kitty's attention. She's probably been messing with each carefully taped and bowed masterpiece anyway, so take a break, grab a spare roll of ribbon, and have a little fun.

Position yourself at one end of the room with kitty at the other. Hold the roll of ribbon up in the air, and let a piece of ribbon dangle from the roll — a good way to entice your kitten. Let it wiggle in the air, then get ready for action!

Hold the end of the ribbon firmly in your finger, then take the ribbon roll, and with your best bowling technique, roll it across the room towards your kitten. She'll chase after it or pounce on the roll, but the fun doesn't stop there. Once the ribbon is unrolled across the room, begin to wiggle your end up and down, creating a rippling effect along the length of the ribbon. Now your ribbon has become wriggling snake, undulating across the room. Kitty won't be able to resist and will pounce and chase after it.

## STUFF ON A STRING

Dangling string games are great for your youngest kitties, but once kittens are a bit older and have developed some strength and coordination, they'll be ready for new challenges and excitement. The games in this section keep kittens firmly grounded in familiar territory, associating playtime with tantalizing strings. But these games also introduce a new element — namely stuff, which you attach and then dangle, flip, bounce, and roll on the string — all to the delight of your growing bundle of fluff. Kittens will hone their stalking, pouncing, and tumbling skills as they graduate (with honors, of course) to mastering these toddler-level amusements.

# Yo-Yo Mouse

Now you see him — now you don't. Try and catch the mousey! Even if you've never been a master of the yo-yo, this is a game that's sure to get your hyper-kitten's attention.

A mouse goes up, a mouse goes down, and kitten tries to grab it. The trick is keeping the stuffed mouse away from your kitten's lightning paws. This game might be more of a challenge for you! Who's faster — you or your kitten?

## What You'll Need

- A piece of strong string, about two feet long
- A generous supply of fat, plush mice

## How It Works

Dangle a soft, stuffed mouse, which you've secured to the end of a string, in front of your eager kitten. Jerk the mouse up, and then drop it down, always just out of kitty's reach. You control the action with a flick of the wrist, right before your kitten's nose.

Kittens can't resist the fast, darting action you create by popping the string and making the mouse leap and twirl elusively. Then let the mouse dangle, tantalizingly, in front of the kitten's nose. Kitty'll play possum, but so will you. Be ready to jerk the string up when you see her paw flash out as she tries to nab that annoying mouse. And every so often, let her win. After all, she's just a kitten.

Make sure to tie your mouse securely to the string — you don't want to spoil the illusion and have your flying mouse suddenly drop dead on the floor.

# Rodeo Mouse and Cowboy Kitten!

Yeehiii! Round 'em up! Time to pull on your cowboy boots and smooth the crease in your Stetson. The rodeo has come to town, and your kitten's the star attraction.

It appears that the mice have been strayin' agin', pardner, and kitten's got to get busy.

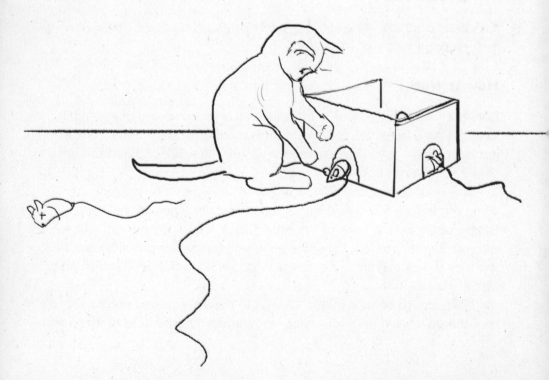

## What You'll Need

- Six to ten stuffed mice tied to long pieces of string
- An open-topped cardboard box to use as your holding pen
- Optional gear: mini-cowboy hat, boots, kitty-chaps, bandanna

## How It Works

Assemble a large herd of toy mice in your rodeo holding pen (a small card-board box, with cut-out gates, works nicely for this purpose).

Make sure each mouse has been lassoed with a good length of string before you assemble them in their pen. Place the holding pen in the middle of the floor, making sure your kitten is watching. Next, begin pulling on the strings, moving each mouse out of the pen and across the floor.

If your kitten is alert, he'll pounce before the mouse gets too far — but wait! — another one's coming! Pretty soon the whole herd will be movin' out as you pull their strings in different directions. Your kitten won't know which way to turn as she pounces here and there, trying to contain the errant mice.

Once your cowboy kitten locates and nabs a mouse, you can help her herd the mouse back to its pen by pulling on the string. When all the mice are safe and sound, reward your kitten with a scratch on the head or a little treat (sorry, no chewin' tabacky fer these cowpokes) — before the mice start moving again.

Oh, no! Saddle up! They're headin' fer the river!

# Catnip Pull

Here's another string-chase game, with the irresistible lure of catnip thrown in for a bonus. Cats always love to sniff, lick, and roll in the 'nip, but this game makes them work for it. Hey, before you know it, they're going to get hooked on the wacky weed, anyway. You may as well introduce them to the good stuff!

## What You'll Need

- A bag of catnip (Select a premium grade herb — quality does vary — so be choosy about your catnip.)
- A selection of stuffable toys with plastic zippers or Velcro closures
- A selection of catnip filled toys (optional)

## How It Works

Roll out your reliable string and tie the catnip toy on securely. You're going to be dragging this thing through the house, so make sure you've triple-knotted it. Now drag the toy along the floor, tantalizing your kitten. Make it stop, then go, let it wiggle and twirl, and watch your kitty go wild.

Hide it under a chair or an ottoman, and watch him try to grab it. If you're up to it (and your hallways can take it), jog through the house, pulling the string behind you. Kitten will be after you and the toy like a shot, racing along the floor, stalking and pouncing.

As always, make sure you let kitty score some satisfying wins, and allow him the chance to savor the sweet taste and smell of his victory.

Keep it simple with a bag of catnip and a sock, or you can purchase any number of hollow toys such as mice or long, plush, bright-orange carrots that are designed to be filled with catnip.

# FASCINATION GAMES

This will come as no surprise to anyone who has spent more than a few minutes in the company of a feline friend: cats like to sit, and cats like to stare (at what is anyone's guess — usually a fluttering bird or a chipmunk twitching his tail in a neighbor's distant yard). And they can gaze for hours.

Sometimes, however, indoor cats run out of interesting things to stare at. The solution? The fascinating activities in this section provide a variety of mesmerizing moments designed to enthrall, intrigue, and generally delight your baby cat — even on a rainy day when there's nothing on TV, and none of the other neighborhood kittens can come over to play.

# Gone Fishin'

Kitties enjoy staring at water almost as much as they love watching birds flying and squirrels playing in the yard (see following games). This diversion gives them the best of both entertainments — and they even get to wash their little paws while they're at it.

## What You'll Need

- A kitten-size plastic bowl (plastic is usually a safer bet than glass or china)
- Floating toys! Use anything that works: corks, rubber bathtub toys, or bobbing plastic flowers.

## How It Works

First, fill a large bowl with water and place it on any nonporous, level surface you don't mind getting wet. Next, place a few tempting, floatable toys into the bowl. Rubber mice, corks, even plastic bugs work — anything that will bob and float in the water.

Introduce your kitten to the water-filled bowl by splashing your fingers in it. Flick the toys around a bit yourself, just to give your kitten the idea. Let kitten watch you having all the fun, then sit back and let kitty take over. She'll splash and fish, knocking the toys around in the water and trying to scoop them out. Join in yourself, and flick the toys around the bowl, back and forth to kitty.

If your intrepid fishercat manages to snag a cork or a bug, be ready with a few replacements. Toss a few more toys into the bowl to keep the game going and your kitten on high alert.

# Pinwheel on a Stick

Movement of any kind fascinates cats and turns on their hunting instinct. Kittens, of course, are just discovering and developing their stalking skills, but like their adult counterparts, they love to watch things flicker and move. They'd probably prefer a butterfly or a little bug, but a colorful, flashing pinwheel makes kitties happy as well.

## What You'll Need

- A plastic pinwheel available at most novelty or toy stores
- A small table fan, — if you're feeling breathless
- A plastic flowerpot filled with sand or dirt or a Styrofoam florist's block

## How It Works

Like the other fascination games described here, this one doesn't require your kitten to do much except pay attention — and maybe space out. You'll need a colorful plastic pinwheel, a place to secure it if you use a fan, and something to make it twirl.

*Option number one:* Hold the pinwheel in front of the kitten, blow on the blades, and the pinwheel twirls.

*Option number two*: Use a small table fan to do the work for you. Set the fan on low, then sit back to watch. Your kitty will enjoy the spinning show, and perhaps she'll paw at the moving object in front of her. The electric fan makes supervision mandatory for this activity!

*Option number three*: Set up the pinwheel outside in a flower box, so the wind catches the blades. Let kitten sit in the window and watch — if the sun is shining on the blades, a light show becomes part of the action!

# I'm Forever Chasing Bubbles

Okay, kitties! Time for your bubble bath!

Ha. Fat chance. No self-respecting kitten would ever voluntarily take that plunge — baths aren't exactly on their list of favorite activities — but bubbles are another story. Kittens love chasing them and watching them float through the air as much as children do.

## What You'll Need

- Bubble solution and a blowing wand
- Sufficient lung power to blow bubbles

## How It Works

You've probably blown bubbles before, so the technique should be familiar.

Dip your wand in the bubble bottle, then carefully pull the wand out of the bottle and blow. A slow, steady breath usually works best and produces the biggest bubbles. You can also wave your wand through the air, letting a stream of smaller bubbles float out behind you.

Sure, that sounds like fun for you, but what does the kitten get out of it? The bubbles, of course, delight cats too, and kitties will chase the soapy orbs through the air watching as they float toward the floor.

Some kitties like to pounce when the bubbles are within striking distance; others prefer simply to stare and follow the path of the bubble, waiting for it to land gently on the floor.

Try blowing bubbles of various sizes and shapes (long bananas or tiny spheres) and sending them in different directions — or treat your kitty to a trip back in time. Pick up a bottle of catnip-flavored bubble solution, designed especially for kitties. Cats love the aroma, of course, and they'll have twice as much fun sniffing and watching all the cool sizes and shapes drifting into the air. Kookamunga Catnip Bubbles are a good choice and are available at most large pet supply stores.

So let your kitten groove on bubbles, man! Toss in a catnip kick and turn on the Moody Blues — she'll be partying like it's 1969!

# Birdies Through a Window

Your kitten probably has already figured this one out on her own, but just in case the outside action is a little slow, you can keep kitty on her toes and encourage your feathered friends to drop by for a visit.

## What You'll Need

- Bird seed! Yes, that's what will lure those blue jays, sparrows, and squawking crows to fly and flutter in front of the window.
- A kitty cushion or window perch

## How It Works

Set up a bird feeder, if you don't have one in your yard already, and fill it with sunflower seeds. You can also simply spread bird seed out on the lawn or on the railing of your deck.

Set up a nice viewing area for kitten and invite (or place) him in front of the window once the birds start to arrive. The neighborhood birds will send out the signal that dinner is served, and your fluttering guests will congregate outside the window.

Guaranteed your kitten will enjoy the show — at least until the bird seed runs out. And he won't want to change the channel.

# Squirrel Surprise

Who's going to get the bigger surprise — the squirrel or your kitten? In this variation of Birdies Through a Window, nuts and seeds are used as payment for a squirrel show — an exclusive engagement for your kitten.

## What You'll Need

- The right food
- A comfortable kitten perch

## How It Works

We use the same technique to attract the squirrels as we did the birds — placing food outside near a good interior kitten-viewing perch.

Windowsills or deck railings work well as nut trays and will bring the squirrels (or chipmunks) closer. Arrange the food (chances are, if you're playing the bird seed game, the local squirrels will have already caught on to the free handouts), and wait for the squirrels to arrive.

Squirrels really like nuts, of course, so if your kitten prefers to watch an occasional all-rodent review, you may want to vary the type of food you use for a squirrel surprise from the seeds you set out to attract the local robins, sparrows, and blue jays.

Your kitten will be delighted by the squirrel parade — and the squirrels will probably be equally thrilled at getting a chance to feast at this beggars' banquet.

# HOLD ON & NEVER LET GO!

They're everywhere! Kittens on the curtains, kittens on your legs, kittens clutching anything they can grab with their sharp tiny claws. Are these furry little demons truly possessed? Of course not — they're just being kittens. And if you've ever watched cats in full hunting mode, you'll know that when they catch prey, the claw and clutch instinct makes perfect sense — they hold on until whatever it is they've managed to grab stops moving.

For indoor cats this instinct is rarely satisfied. Maybe they may manage to catch a stray mouse or two or a juicy bug in the summer, but that's not enough to satisfy their clutch 'n kill desires; hence, the shredded curtains, pillows, and furniture arms — not to mention all those vulnerable body parts of the kitty's hapless, bloodied human.

The following games will help kitty satisfy his natural Jack-the-Ripper urge, without causing you or your furnishings unnecessary pain and damage.

# Rassle the Tassel

What's more tempting than a bushy-tailed squirrel? Well, a simple-to-make fluttering tassel may be just the answer.

## What You'll Need

- A large pincushion (without the pins, of course) or small novelty pillow (sewing supply stores are good sources.)
- Dangling materials to enhance your tassel: Ribbons, string, whatever works to cover the cushion

## How It Works

You'll be tempting (okay, taunting) your kitten with a fat, soft, wiggly lump, and the object is to get kitty to pounce, then work her claw-clutch magic.

You'll need something that's eye-catching yet annoying enough to raise your kitten's hackles. A plump little pillow or a large pincushion serves the purpose nicely. But to make it attractive enough to earn kitty's claws, you'll have to get creative. Cover the pincushion with dangling strings or ribbons attached securely with thread or nontoxic "superglue." Attach a long string from the center so you can dangle the object, and now you've got a giant tassel.

Try dangling it in front of your kitten or dragging it across the floor. Let the ribbons tickle her belly and ears or flutter in front of her face — you're not playing keep-away; you want your kitten to catch it. If the object is the right size, kitty will grab it and dig in, kicking her back feet and curling her body around the tassel.

Try moving it while she has it in her clutches — she'll work even harder, making sure it doesn't get away. And if you make a few tassels of different sizes and shapes, you'll keep kitty interested in this game, instead of in the sofa and the carpets.

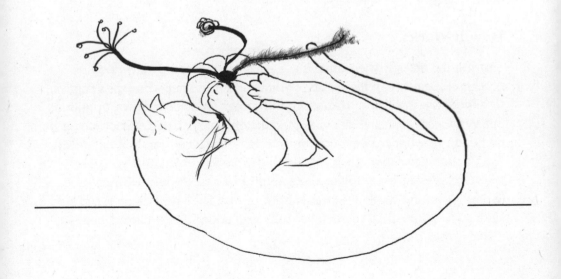

# Clutch and Kill (not really!)

Yes, dear cat lovers, we must admit it: kitties like to kill things. Maybe they've been hanging around humans too long, but cats don't seem to be satisfying that ancient survival instinct to kill just for food anymore; cats have made a game of hunting.

Clutch and Kill lets them have their fun, without turning the "fun" into a blood sport.

## What You'll Need

- A selection of large, annoying-looking stuffed toys (clowns and Teddy bears do the trick for our cats.)
- One or two thick and sturdy hand-puppets

## How It Works

Trot out this activity when kitten is in a particularly blood-thirsty mood or, conversely, beat her to the punch (or claw) and rouse her when she's napping.

There are three basic choices for this game: Teddy bear, clown, or puppet. With teddy bear, the idea is to make kitten jealous. Cuddle Teddy, stroke his head, and whisper sweet nothings into his little stuffed ear: *Ooh, nice Teddy. Teddy's such a good boy! Look, kitty, isn't Teddy precious?* Now that you've set the stage, present Teddy to your irate kitten. Make sure you're wearing your leather glove, and wiggle the bear in front of kitty. She'll pounce on it and start kicking, giving it all she's got with her back legs, pounding the hapless bear until it finally stops moving.

Gently pull the bear from kitten's claws — she'll hold on and, of course, she'll win. This will, we guarantee, be most satisfying for your kitten.

Use the same basic technique with the clown, except kitten won't be jealous of clowns – clowns are just annoying. And since most kittens display a unique animosity toward clowns, this game is always a winner. Wiggle the grinning, garish doll and imitate a clown's creepy, high-pitched giggle: Hah, hah, hah! Hah, hah, hah!! Look at the sweet little kitty! Rest assured, kitten won't fall for clown's phony flattery — this bozo will soon be history.

With hand puppet, of course, you're presenting a moving target. Take care to wear protective gear — thick sweatshirts, gloves, etc. Then get that puppet moving!

Scoring for this game is fairly simple:

Kitten — 3

Teddy, clown & puppet — 0

# Kitten Caboose

Turn your playroom or hallway into a Kitty-Kiddie Park as you take your little engineer for a ride on the rug train express!

## What You'll Need

- An old scatter rug or carpet remnant, suitable for pulling
- A room or a hallway with a smooth floor to serve as your track
- Matching Casey Jones caps for you and your kitty (optional)
- All the bells and whistles

## How It Works

We all remember the thrill of our first ride on an amusement park's minia-ture train. There we were, sitting proudly in our seats, waving as Mom & Dad cheered us on; the tiny train chugging along past fake windmills and railroad depots, tooting its eardrum-piercing whistle and grinding to a sudden halt after a kid fell off the back.

Well, now your kitten can experience the same joy and excitement you did as a child when you invite her aboard the rug train express!

First, get her attention with a *toot! toot!* whistle sound and begin pulling your scatter rug down the hall. When kitty's ready to play, she'll hop aboard and hang on for the ride. Pull her slowly (you don't want to lose her) up and down the hall or around the room. Keep tooting! or making a cool chugging sound as your rug train clatters along, with Kitten Caboose bringing up the rear, flicking her tail with delight.

Cats love to glide around the room with their humans providing the power. Once kitty gets the hang of this one, she'll start the action, and when she wants to play, she'll be waiting for you at the station, sitting on the rug, ready for you to shovel the coal and fire up the engine!

# PART TWO:
# Adult Entertainment

Now that your kitty is all grown up, it's time for you and Mr. Mature to enjoy more sophisticated entertainment. Face it: he's not a clinging kitten anymore — heck, by now he's probably moved into his own kitty condo — so it's time to engage his interest with new and challenging activities that will keep him active, alert, and in top cat shape.

It's a good idea to engage in active playtime with your indoor cat for about 15 minutes two or three times a day. If you play a few of the games listed here each day, you'll look forward to these play sessions with the same enthusiasm as kitty. Then you'll both be tuckered out, Mr. Mature will be satisfied, and you won't feel guilty snoozing with him on the sofa for the rest of the evening.

# WORKOUT!

Weight-loss activities and exercise are essential for an indoor cat's good health. Outdoor cats are always on the prowl, hunting and chasing prey, so fighting the Battle of the Kitty Bulge isn't a problem for the local neighborhood tomcat. Indoor cats, however, need regular physical activity to help maintain a healthy weight. They may chase down the occasional mouse or bug, but they'll need more activities to keep them moving than setting off on the weekly mouse safari.

Although this book doesn't include a kitty aerobics CD, the activities in this chapter will help your cat get his daily workout. The following games are designed to keep your bustling bundle of fur movin', groovin', and healthy.

# Flashlight Romp

Light up your kitty's life with some high-beam fun! Here's a workout your cat will take a shine to.

## What You'll Need

- A flashlight with a good, powerful beam
- A darkened or dimly lit room

## How It Works

This game is the original Laser Sprite (see next section) — the difference is in the equipment. Use a flashlight to project an enticing beam of light in a dimly lit space. The smaller Maglites work well for this activity — they project a more focused beam of light – but any flashlight will do. Your cat will chase the light wherever you shine it. Since it's a workout game, try running kitty up and down the stairs, through a cat tunnel, or around some strategically placed chairs or footstools.

The advantage to using a flashlight vs. the laser beam is safety. The laser requires more control since you must keep it away from the cat's eyes. (Some people prefer not to use a laser at all exactly for that reason.) Flashlight Romp, lets your kitty run wild. He can cross in and out of the beam, running fast, working off those extra Pounces.

No scoring needed for this game — just fun for you and Mr. Trim.

# Crazy Susan

For families at the dinner table, this spinning food-delivery device is a convenient energy saver. But for today's active aerobic cat, it's an essential piece of exercise equipment.

## What You'll Need

- A good variety of intriguing toys – all shapes, styles, and sizes
- A sturdy plastic or wooden lazy Susan, available at most kitchen stores
- A few tasty treats (optional)

## How It Works

Place your lazy Susan on the floor and arrange a tempting selection of toys on top of the wheel. Variety is the spice of this lively game, so mix in fresh catnip sacks, plush mice, rolling balls, and wispy feathers. If kitty's not on a serious diet, add a few treats (we'll call them cat-power bars) to the wheel, along with the toys. Let's face it: they're not as fattening as some of those energy drinks, so you don't have to feel too guilty.

Once the toys are arranged for maximum effect, let the fun begin. Start spinning the lazy Susan, slowly at first, as your cat watches the toys and treats whirling around and around. She may try to swat them off the wheel, or she may try to pounce. Either way, she'll be after those toys, and chances are, the toys will soon be airborne. So watch out! This game gets pretty crazy!

As kitty gets used to the spinning wheel, try moving it a little faster. Cats enjoy staring, then pouncing, as the wheel turns around. Your cat may even try moving the lazy Susan herself. However cats choose to engage with this game, they'll be active, alert, and workin' out!

Power to the kitties!

# Teeter-Totter Tumble

What cat doesn't enjoy a good old-fashioned seesaw? Okay, probably most cats don't, but that's only because they've never tried one. Once you introduce them to this game, your kitties will be falling all over themselves.

## What You'll Need

• A round log or a sturdy, thick cardboard roll, about three feet long, with a six to eight inch diameter
• A wooden plank, about five feet long and 18 inches wide
• Assorted cat toys, balls, and string

## How It Works

Assemble your seesaw — it's a cinch! Simply place your log or cardboard roll on the floor and balance the plank on top of it. The plank should be centered on the log for maximum seesaw action.

Next, place and/or attach some tempting toys to one end of the plank. (Secure some or all of the toys to the plank. Tie or thumbtack the string to the board on both ends. Then tie your toys onto the string.)

Now, lower the kitty end of the plank to the floor, and the toys will be sitting or dangling from the end of the plank that's in the air. Time to bring in kitty!

Introduce kitty to the seesaw and show her the toy display. Wiggle the toys to arouse her interest, and roll a few balls down the plank. Then move her onto the other end of the plank. It may take a few tries, but eventually your cat will walk the plank to go after the toys. When she does, the seesaw action begins. Once the toy end of the plank goes down, move the toys up to the other end, which will now be in the air.

# Mouse Toss!

Relive your glory days shootin' hoops while kitty gets a workout.

## What You'll Need

- A basket, a bag, or a cardboard box, deep enough to keep the mice from bouncing out
- A good supply of soft, stuffed mice. The fatter ones work best for this game.

## How It Works

This game requires a bit of skill from both you and your cat.

The idea is for you to toss stuffed mice into a container (any box, basket, or bag will do) placed several feet across the room. Kitty's job is to block the shot and/or go after the mice that have either landed in the basket for a score (Three points! Why not?) or skidded across the floor after you've shot an air-ball.

The scoring is simple: three points for you for each shot you make; three points for the cat if she blocks it.

Our cat has caught on to this game and enjoys the challenge. He waits for the shot, blocks it like a pro, and usually ends up winning, displaying his pleasure with the kitty equivalent of the high five: tail up, smug and sassy.

Calorie burn? Hard to measure, but this game definitely keeps our Maine coon active.

# Ping-Pong Paws

Every executive cat enjoys a brisk workout at the club after a hard day of mousing. This game gives your mighty mouse-winner a chance to unwind (and lose some weight) after a long day in the jungle.

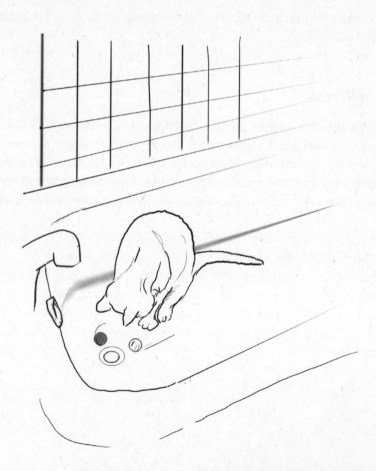

## What You'll Need

- A bathtub
- Ping-pong balls

## How It Works

The playing court is your own clean, dry bathtub. A deeper tub makes it easier to keep the ball in play — and to keep your kitty moving.

Step one is to remove all obstacles from the tub: soap, conditioner, your rubber duck — anything that will slow kitty down or interfere with the ball's movement.

Once you and your cat are ready to play, place kitty (never force him, of course) in the bathtub. Toss a ball in the air or bounce it off the wall to ramp up the excitement. Then throw a ball in the tub and let it bounce. Your cat will go after it, trying to trap it with his claws. Since ping-pong balls are hard to grasp (at least, if you don't have thumbs), the ball and cat will keep moving. If the game starts to slow down, throw in another ball or two and watch things get really wild. The balls will bounce and roll around the tub, careening off the sides and popping into the air as your cat goes after them, scrambling and leaping.

Scoring? Nah — it's a workout game. If you want to keep your cat happy and svelte, try this game; it's one he'll want to keep on playing.

# Ice Cube Hockey

Look out! Kitty is about to deliver a wicked slapshot that that will get his opponent's attention. But this isn't overtime in the NHL — it's dinnertime, when cats usually engage in faceoffs around the food bowl and not on arena ice over a tasteless hockey puck.

If you'd like to help kitty channel that aggression with a good, fast-paced game (and in a less combative manner), read on. No high-sticking or high-clawing allowed.

## What You'll Need

- A bowl of ice
- A cardboard box to serve as the net
- A floor with a smooth surface and plenty of room
- Painter's tape (optional)

## How It Works

The rules are similar to a real hockey game: for each goal you score a point. Of course, like most games you play with your cat, there really aren't any rules, and if there were, your cat would change them. But that doesn't mean you can't try.

Set up your hockey rink, establishing goal lines, a center line, and boundaries with your painter's tape, if you wish (the walls of your room may serve a similar purpose). Don't worry about regulation specs; dimensions are dependent on the size of your room, and with this game, the more floor space you have, the better. Establish two goal areas at either end of the room. Your cardboard box, cut in half, will serve as your goal nets.

Start the game by placing an ice cube puck on the center line, then flicking it with your finger toward a goal. Kitty will pounce at the slippery cube and knock it back toward you or against the wall or maybe even toward your goal.

Watch out! It's a power play! Kitty's on the move!

You and your cat can take turns playing offense and defense and acting as goalie. Either way, once you put the ice puck in play, your cat will be actively engaged. Now it's your turn to take a whack at the cube and try to send it past kitty. See if you can score a goal – but don't get overconfident – cats are excellent defenders. And your cat may surprise you, scoring a few goals himself. (Cats, of course, are famous for their hat tricks.)

The object, sort of, is to score goals, but you'll both have fun just knocking the ice cube around the floor. When it melts down to a small size, bring out a fresh cube and start the action again. Kitty will be ready for more, pouncing and swatting at the frozen puck while you flick it back at him, feinting, checking, and scoring!

# Roller Can Derby

Every rough 'n' tumble cat will appreciate this feline version of the arena classic that leaves audiences cheering, wincing, and breathless. Your cat will cheer, too, when you roll out his favorite roller can and begin to play this one. No knee or elbow pads required.

## What You'll Need

- An empty can or two, with plastic lids
- A few small stones
- One or two cats, ready for action

## How It Works

Movement and sound are intriguing to cats, and this game features both in abundance. The object of the game is to roll an empty can (which contains a few pebbles) across the floor before your cat can stop you. Don't expect to win this game — if you're a gambler, bet on kitty.

The can should be empty except for a few small stones which you've tucked inside. Secure the stones in the can with a tight plastic lid, and you've got your roller can.

Time to begin the derby.

Rattle the can a few times to signal your cat that it's time to play. You'll need a good-sized space and, preferably, a smooth floor surface. Begin at one end of the room, rolling the can with your foot toward the other side of the space.

Be prepared: your cat will not let you advance. He will pounce at the can, intrigued (or irritated) by the rattling stones, and he will knock the can off its course. Once this occurs, you must, of course, begin again. Kitty will be waiting.

If two or more cats are on the kitty team, your chances of victory grow even slimmer. The cats will be sliding and tumbling all over themselves, knocking the can every whichway but toward your wall. Once again, you're the loser. Don't be too hard on yourself. Delight in your cats' courage and dexterity. In your heart you know you're a winner.

If multiple cats are playing this game, they may forget about you altogether, taking over the game themselves and knocking the rattling can all around the room. Their ignoring you should not damage your fragile self-esteem. Sit back, enjoy your cats and let them play. Be glad you escaped without a shredded toe. Cheer on your champion kitties.

# TECHNO GAMES

Although a kitty joystick has yet to appear on pet store toy shelves, that doesn't mean your cat doesn't want one. After all, he's seen you or your companion V.G.A. (video game addict) staring at that blinking, dancing screen for hours, operating the little stick device with glazed eyes and slack-jawed fascination.

Why wouldn't he want one? All cats, as we know, appreciate the benefits of mind-numbing mesmerism. Unfortunately, their lack of thumbs puts kitties at a significant disadvantage when it comes to using the latest version of Xbox or Gameboy.

But thumbs or no thumbs, today's techno-savvy millennial mewers belong to a group like no other. They've been born into a world ruled by high-tech gadgetry (you may assume they are utterly dependent on that automatic kibble dispenser you bought them for Christmas last year), so they expect and, yes, deserve the same kind of state-of-the-art diversions we've been frittering away the dwindling minutes of our own lives on for the past 30 years.

So it's time to bring your cat into the 21st century and let him fritter away his time, too. Sure, he could be spending his days reading T.S. Eliot or inventing a better mousetrap, but remember: cats have nine lives — they can afford to blow a few.

# Motor Mouse and His Robot Friends

Gentlemice, start your engines! They're off! And kitty is after them with an undisguised, savage glee.

Admittedly, these toys come off the shelf of the pet store or from your favorite Web site. But your kitty needs to stay current to be able to compete in today's cat-eat-cat, take-no-prisoners rat race, especially if breadwinning involves chasing mice — or rats.

So your contemporary cat will be thrilled to face, chase, and even embrace this new technology as he hones his hunting skills, stalking, pouncing, and racing after the battery-powered demons described below.

## What You'll Need

- Motor mice: there are a variety of choices available via the e-marketplace
- Robospiders: remote-controlled spidery toys, also sold on the Web
- Basket kitten: available at most big retail stores, this cat sleeps, breathes, and purrs

## Where to Purchase

- Motor mice:
  www.smarthome.com/46304.html
  www.amazon.com/Incredible-Motor-Mouse-Cat-Toy/dp/
  B000633R4C
  www.kennelvet.com/motor-mouse-cat-toy-bonus-kit-p-2609.html
  www.drsfostersmith.com

- Cyberspider, bugs, & robotics:
  www.wowwee.com/

- Basket Kitty:
  www.thisplaceisazoo.com/cats.html
  Any big box retail store (Target, etc.)

## How It Works

Basically, you tempt, taunt and tantalize kitty with an array of inventive, self-propelled toys that can be purchased from any number of retailers and e-tailers.

Begin with motor mice, which can be as simple as a windup toy or as sophisticated as a remote-controlled, battery-operated furball, equipped with all the
bells, microchips, and whistles.

Get kitty's attention by powering up the thing and letting it charge across
the room. Kitty may pounce and kill or run and hide. Her reaction is dependent, of course, on her inherent level of caution or lack thereof. Do not be
deterred if, at first, kitty behaves like a mewling wimp — she'll get over it.
Curiosity will win the day, so keep that gigademon moving.

Introduce a second mouse or even a third for added excitement. If the
toys are remote-controlled, grab a human partner and try racing the mice
across the room. Which mouse will win before kitty pounds the hell out it?
Your skill using the mouse remote will improve along with kitty's ability to
chase and intercept the thing.

Another technique is to hide the motor mice under a chair or behind a
door. Get kitty's attention by slightly moving the mouse using your remote,
but don't engage in an all-out scamper across the floor. Your cat will assume
the position: waiting and watching. . . . Squeeak! Here comes the mouse and
there goes kitty!

Now add a little twist with the variations below.

## The Cyberbug Variation:

If you opt to purchase cyberbugs, add these into the mix. Spiders, a popular
choice, skitter and crawl across the floor, imitating the moves of real spiders.
They look like spider robots (and not the real thing), but they are as much fun
as the motor mice and add another level of interest to all the robots you've
got running around on the floor. Since these toys don't move in the same way
as the mice do, your cat will be enticed anew and eager to take on this
challenge.

# Romantic Sleeping Kitty:

Finally, for a more passive techno-choice, let your cat meet the sleeping kitten. These charming, battery-powered friends look and act like real kittens (sleeping puppies are also available) sleeping in a basket. Flip the switch on the bottom and kitten comes to life, breathing and purring in her little basket. They don't do much else, so you'll want to use these toys sparingly and only when your cat needs a new diversion. Set them up when your kitty's not around, and let him discover his new friend on his own. He may or may not want to play with it, but at the very least, it will get his attention.

Single cats who are looking for love may want to snuggle up to the little robocat and fall asleep, dreaming of long walks in the park, tails entwined, and sharing bowls of kibble. If you see your cat being drawn into these romantic flights of fancy, don't be alarmed. All cats enjoy an active fantasy life, so it's perfectly normal. However, if kitty spends an inordinately unhealthy amount of time mooning over basket kitty, it may be time to visit the local animal rescue shelter and bring him home the real thing.

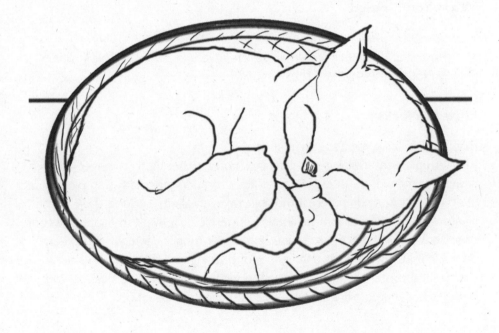

# Screen Savior

Let kitty worship the techno-gods on your computer screen — while you take an old-fashioned nap. This one doesn't require much human effort or interaction, but it's perfect for those inevitable moments when your cat is desperate for a good game of anything and all you want to do is flop facedown on the couch. You've been praying for this one!

## What You'll Need

- A computer with at least a 15-inch screen
- A variety of computer screensavers, available and downloadable online, from various cat-loving Web sites

## How It Works

Point and click — yes, it's really that easy.

Set up an entertaining, eye-catching, mouth-watering screensaver on your computer, then let the software do all the work. Whether kitty's an old paw at Web navigation, a computer cat newbie, or even a kitty Luddite, she'll sit for hours watching skittering mice, floating butterflies, wiggling fish, flapping falcons, or speeding shapes race across your computer monitor. Since most screen savers feature an ever-changing variety of dazzling eye candy features, your kitty will be content to follow the action without ever laying a paw on your keyboard or — most important — demanding your attention.

CAUTION: You already know this, but cats have claws, and, yes, an overly curious kitty may scratch your precious computer screen. So wait and watch the first few times you try this one, and see if your cat is a computer mouser. If she goes after the image on the screen, you may want to skip using this game. But then again, computer screens are relatively inexpensive these days — maybe getting a good afternoon snooze is worth it.

# Laser Sprite!

To humans, it's just a spot of intense red light that appears when we press a button on a penlike device — but cats are clearly more imaginative than we are. A cat's mind and eye transforms that simple dot of ruby red (most commonly associated with dull PowerPoint presentations) into a magical, elusive fairy!

## What You'll Need

- A laser pointer, available at most pet or office supply stores
  (Tip: The office models last a lot longer. They're worth the extra money.)
- Room to run. Kitty'll need it!

## How It Works

Aim your laser beam at a wall or on the floor when your kitty least expects it. To get the cat's attention, create an audio signature that kitty will associate with the beam of light. You might try *Oooooh, it's magic dot time! Fairy, fairy, fairy!* or an eerie throat warble that will make any cat's ears twitch with excitement. Then move the light past your cat, making sure he sees it. Pounce! Kitty will be up and running, leaping for the ceiling or bouncing off the walls, trying to trap the beam of light that's always, maddeningly, just beyond his grasp.

Make your laser sprite climb the walls, dance on the ceiling, or scamper across the floor — all the while with kitty in hot pursuit. We guarantee your cat won't get tired of this one, and yes, he'll get a workout!

CAUTION: Those laser beams can damage animal or human eyes. Never point the beam at anyone — cat or person — and keep the beam well away from pouncing, dashing cats.

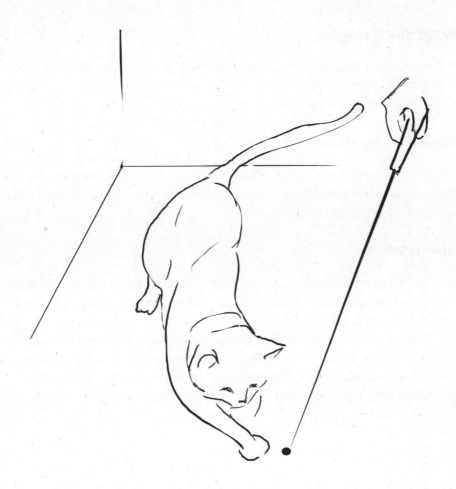

# Saturday Matinee

Lights! Camera! Action!

It's a rainy afternoon, the other cats are catching a few z's, and no humans want to play. What's a restless kitty to do? Well, he can do what all the other kids do when they're bored to tears: pop in a video and chill out on the couch.

## What You'll Need

- Kitty viddies (a.k.a. video entertainment designed exclusively for cats)
- A television and a DVD player
- A digital camcorder (optional)

## Where to Purchase

There is an impressive selection of DVDs available for kitty viewing at Web sites such as www.mewvies.com. A quick Web search for videos for cats will bring you to plenty of resources.

## How It Works

Yeah, yeah. We've all gotten the same tedious finger-wagging advice: "Don't let your TV set be your kittysitter. Do fun activities with your cat; otherwise, he'll turn into a fuzzy couch potato.

Well, since there are dozens of interactive games in this book for you to play with your cat, don't feel guilty about exposing kitty to a little passive entertainment. Cats, as we know, love to sit and stare, so why not let a little technology help you indulge this instinctive kitty urge?

Kitty videos are available from various Web sites, and they include great kitty classic entertainment such as endless shots of scampering squirrels, twittering birds, and crawling, skittering insects. All the stuff your cat wants to watch while kicking back on a lazy afternoon with a nice big bowl of Temptations.

So, pop in the DVD and let kitty start watching. He'll be intrigued (especially if your TV screen is fairly large) and excited by all the outdoor action occurring right inside his house. Let him discover the movie by himself, or bring him over to the screen. Cats can watch these little flicks for hours all by themselves. You can watch along with him if you're as fascinated by tail-waving chipmunks as he is — or you can take a nap.

Another option is to shoot your own film right in your backyard or in the local park. If you have a camcorder with a zoom lens, try your hand at directing a film of your own. Cast robins, crows, squirrels, and bugs. Edit for maximum action effect, or create a moving story line — the sad chipmunk, alone in the woods, finds love at last 'neath an oak tree.

# Tunes For Cats to Groove On

Ladies and gentlemen, kittens and cats, we're delighted once again to present the sophisticated jazz stylings of the original Bird.

So put your paws together for the Common Great-tailed Grackle!

## What You'll Need

- A selection of audio CDs of bird calls and bird songs
- A CD/DVD player
- One or more really cool cats

## Where to Purchase

A large number of Web sites devoted to birds and bird enthusiasts sell audio CDs of bird calls. The following sites have excellent selections:

www.all-birds.com/Sound.htm
www.birdwatching.com/tips/birdsongs.html

Note: Avoid posting announcements on these sites that you're buying the CDs for a cat, or resist the temptation to write reviews of the CDs describing how much your cat loved them. Chances are, bird lovers won't appreciate your efforts.

## How It Works

This is another semipassive activity that will nevertheless intrigue and delight (and perhaps drive a little wild) your nature-loving indoor kitty.

First things first: you'll want to purchase several audio CDs of bird sounds. These are available on a multitude of Web sites devoted to the bird lover. Some of these sites have impressive collections, and you can purchase CDs featuring sounds of birds which inhabit various regions of the country and around the world.

Next, pop in the CD, turn it on, and wait for kitty's reaction. She may rush to the windows or run around, looking for her feathered friends. They may be waiting for her — outside (sorry, Kitty, you're out of luck!), but their sounds will be filling the house, so she'll keep looking. You can also combine this activity with Flying Feathers (see page 74), fluttering the feathers in front of your cat as the bird calls play in the background.

Your cat may find one CD more alluring than another. So try a few and see what sounds she grooves to. Your cat may also fall asleep and simply ignore the sounds. If this occurs, rest assured, kitty will be dreaming of beautiful birds flitting and fluttering in her yard, outside her living room window.

## BELLY UP!

Watch out! Kitty's on her back, and she's armed and dangerous.

Cats like to entice us by flipping onto their backs, looking innocent and playful. Please rub my belly — I'm so sweet. . . . But a cat's idea of fun doesn't always mesh with a human's — especially when your cat thinks clawing your bare hand or arm is the height of entertainment. How many of us have taken the bait, unable to resist our adorable kitty's furry gut, only to find our pitiful, bare, unprotected hand at the mercy of the kitty death grip?

What to do? Sure, you can still play and even take the bait, but arm yourself with a few simple tools, and keep your hand out of the shredder.

And of course, remember to shower your cat with praise after each successful catch.

# Leather Glove Tickle

This neat trick will take your cat by surprise, especially if you've been on the receiving end of a bunch of your kitty's sneak attack death grips.

## What You'll Need

- Leather work gloves
- A cat with claws
- An ounce of courage

## How It Works

Wait for kitty to roll onto her back, and make sure your gloves are handy. Slip on your gloves and purr softy to your cat, *Oooh, what a sweet little kitty! Does Precious want a belly rub?* Sure, play dumb. It's not hard for us. Let's face it, we're only human.

Or you can start the action if you want. Soften kitty up with some nice belly rubs, maybe when she's on her side, snoozing in the evening.

Either way, she'll be playing possum, of course, ready to spring her Venus fly trap claws, but this time you've got protection. Slip on a thick leather glove and keep gently tickling kitty's stomach. When she closes the trap, you won't feel a thing (remember, use thick leather gloves), and she'll really be able to dig in with her claws, which apparently due to her innate huntress-killer instinct is incredibly satisfying.

One note: Cats may get sick of this trick once they catch on — but since clawing hands is really bad behavior, if Miss Precious eventually gives up clawing human flesh, you probably won't be complaining.

# Flying Feathers

It's a bird! It's a plane! It's . . . just a bunch of feathers attached to a flexible plastic wand. But you and kitty can still have fun with these ingenious devices which mimic the actions of a bird.

Some cats enjoy chasing these feathers around the room as you make them fly through the air, but cats also love to lie on their backs, paws and claws waving in the air, trying to snag the phony sparrow.

## What You'll Need

- Plastic wand and feathers (most pet stores sell these in a variety of styles)
- A cat on her back

## How It Works

Use the long, flexible plastic wand to float and fly a bunch of large feathers, which are attached to a plastic string. You control the bird when you wave it through the air; it looks and sounds like a bird (at least it does to a cat — the feathers really flutter), and your big game hunter, of course, wants to catch it.

While your cat's on her back, you can make the bird flap through the air, close to her claws, or even have it gently land on her stomach or chest. Just when she's about to close the claw-trap, make the bird fly away, just out of kitty's clutches.

You'll develop your own technique with the wand, making the feathers dip and twirl through the air. Score one point for you when the bird escapes — if the bird is history, kitty wins one.

# The Elusive Peacock Feather

No, you don't need to raid the local zoo at night. You can buy these long, colorful feathers from the local pet store. The feathers are sold for about a buck apiece, so you can stock up on several. The idea is the same as Flying Feathers. You've basically got a long, flexible stick with an attractive feather on it. You tantalize your cat — your cat clutches the feather in his claws. Not rocket science, but so what? Your cat's not a physics major, is he?

## What You'll Need

- Several peacock feathers
- A standard intolerant cat

## How It Works

Use your peacock feather to tickle kitty's belly and nose, or try wiggling the feather under a chair or popping it out from behind a doorway. These feathers are easy to move (and easier to control than the plastic wand), and if you shake them quickly and let them rest, they seem to mimic the movement of prey that's cleverly hiding. Cats, with their active imaginations, love to pounce on these feathery things, and they enjoy pawing at them while on their backs.

We usually sit in a chair when we're using this toy and tickle our cat's stomach. Forrest, our cat, loves to hate these things, and he can't resist swatting them and trying to grab them.

The long feathers are not as durable as the plastic wand, of course, so they won't last forever. They tend to shred pretty quickly and break in half — but they do provide good cat fun anytime you use them.

# MouseStickle

This game provides a little variety from the usual mouse-toy games (tossing or string pulls), and lets you, once again, keep a safe distance from your piranha cat's razor-sharp claws and teeth.

## What You'll Need

- A sturdy stick
- Two to three feet of nylon fishing line
- A plump, plush mouse or two

## How It Works

Wrap the nylon fishing line around the mouse tightly, so the mouse won't come loose. Then attach the line to the stick. Wait until kitty is on her back, and dangle the mouse in front of her. If she's not interested at first, drag the mouse across the floor using your stick and line and try to attract her attention (or at least get her to open her eyes, if she's grabbing a little catnap). After a few passes, even the most aloof kitty queen will be unable to resist.

Now bounce the mouse up and down, grazing kitty's belly, and if she's sitting up, she'll probably flop over once the game begins. Your cat will enjoy swatting at the mouse and then kicking and grabbing it once it's in her hot, little claws. As she holds on, gently pull the stick up and try to get your mouse back. It's fun playing a little tug-of-war with your MouseStickle, even if you never win.

If your cat lets go, try a workout variation by dragging the mouse across the floor so kitty can chase it. The thin nylon line creates the illusion of a mouse on the loose, with your cat in hot pursuit!

# BATTER UP!

Ah spring! Mouthwatering birds are nesting, tempting baby chipmunks and moles scurry through the yard. And a young cat's fancy turns to . . . baseball — or at least some really good games that owe a tip of the Major League cap to America's favorite pastime.

We shouldn't really expect cats to know how to round the bases or care much about balls and strikes (since when did a cat ever follow the rules about anything?), but cats do enjoy smacking stuff out of the air, especially when the stuff is tossed in their direction.

Batter up! fun will keep your hairy homerun king at the top of his game — just watch out for the neighbor's windows.

# Toss 'n' Swat

Hey, batter-batter-batter! Hey batter-batter-batter!

Kitties come running, ready to play ball! when they hear this ballpark announcement. And there's no need for trips to the mall for fancy sports shoes or protective gear — your hairy shortstop is already equipped with built-in claw-cleats and perfectly padded paw-mitts.

## What You'll Need

- Stuff to toss: corks, paper balls, toy mice, or ping-pong balls
- Your furry slugger
- Peanuts and Cracker Jacks (optional)

## How It Works

Kitty's in the batter's box (seated on a chair), and Mom and Dad are both ace pitchers. The ball? Use any light, safe object you can toss through the air, and pitch it toward your kitty. Kitty, of course, will be keeping his eye on the "ball" and trying to whack it out of the park with his paw. Your job is to whiz it past him.

Verbally signal before each pitch with an excited *Get ready! One, two, three!* before tossing the ball to keep your swinger on high alert and fully engaged in the action.

Underhand tosses seem to work best since you're really not trying to win this game — the fun is watching your superstar cat hit a triple or a homer. So give Joltin' Jo-Jo a chance, pitch it slowly, and aim for his little strike zone.

# Pitch 'n' Catch

Another ballgame for your all-star cat, designed to play with soft toys only.

## What You'll Need

- A large array of soft, stuffed toys, suitable for tossing
- A cat with claws

## How It Works

The setup's the same as Toss 'n' Swat — keep kitty on a level playing field, sitting on a chair or table. Assemble a good selection of soft toys. You can use anything with a little weight to it, so that it sails enticingly through the air. Simple balls you make yourself out of yarn are equally effective.

Gently lob the toy toward your cat. The toy arcs through the air and, instead of batting it as in Toss 'n' Swat, kitty tries to catch it. Cats love to snag the soft toys on their claws (usually impossible when you're tossing corks and ping pong balls). Chances are, though, they won't play catch and release, so don't expect a toss back.

The rules? Cat makes a catch — cat wins. See how many catches he can make in a row.

Depending upon your cat's mood, this game may turn into a version of Toss 'n' Swat. No matter — let your cat decide. The object is to have fun, so enjoy whatever game your kitty's in the mood for.

Who knows? At the end of the season, he might win the Golden Paw Award.

# Paper Ball Pop-ups

Of course, every Major League kitty loves to bat and catch, but cats also like to chase those errant pop-ups and skidding ground balls all around the infield. Compact paper balls fit the bill nicely for this game, and you can make them yourself from a few sheets of newspaper or typing paper.

## What You'll Need

- A good supply of paper balls
- Room to run
- One or more wacky kitties

## How It Works

It's game day, and your sultan of swat needs a little infield practice. Be prepared with plenty of paper balls — they'll be flying all over the place once kitty takes the field.

Send your cat fielder out between second and third base, or if you're practicing with the whole team, assign each cat a position (okay, they'll probably assign themselves) — sofa leg, table, and ottoman work pretty well for our cats and gives them something to hide behind as they wiggle in anticipation.

Start flinging the balls across the floor, trying to send them past your kitty. He'll try to grab them, but if a ball rolls past your cat — watch out! He'll be chasing the ball and knocking it across the floor, determined to nab it. (Often this game turns into a soccer match, especially if you're fielding multiple kitties.)

And since variety is the spice of any cat's life, keep him alert in the infield by throwing large, medium, and mini-balls his way — guaranteed you'll keep him hopping.

## Volleyball Smackdown!

A variation on the Batter Up!-themed games, Volleyball Smackdown lets kitty swat stuff with her paw and get supreme catisfaction from delivering a solid, well-timed smack!

## What You'll Need

- A good variety of small cat toys and balls. (Ping-pong balls are ideal, as are — for the oenophile cat — a wine bottle cork. Our cat loves to whack corks out of the air, even when he's sober.)
- A net barrier that you create out of a cardboard box or a soft cushion

## How It Works

Set up a little barrier that will serve as your volleyball net. A ping-pong table with a little net would be the ultimate court for this kitty game, but you don't need anything fancy.

Once you've gathered the players on the court, toss the ball up fairly high, so that it flies up and over the net. A higher toss works best for this game since it allows your cat time to follow the ball in the air and get set for the smackdown.

The object of this game can be to keep the ball in the air as you hit it back and forth across the net. But what cats seem to like better is smashing the ball out of the air once you toss it to them.

If you manage to hit the ball and keep it aloft, well, score one for you. But cats, with their quicksilver reflexes and accurate aim, usually swat the ball down and over the net before your sluggish human responses can manage a save.

Prepare to lose.

# THE GREAT INDOORS

A surefire method for keeping your indoor cats lively and entertained is to create variety in their everyday environments. Something as simple as a wicker basket that had been occupying the far corner of the living room for years, placed unexpectedly in the center of your kitchen, can keep kitties intrigued for hours. How did THAT get there? Whatever it is, I have to jump inside it! An empty paper grocery bag left open and standing in the middle of a room generates a similar response and is another tried-and-true winner. Simple surprises like these are always fun, but you can also keep kitty entertained by creating environments that are a bit more elaborate than the old surprise bag-in-the-hallway stunt. With a little imagination and some strategically placed items that will arouse a cat's interest, you can create mini-kitty wonderlands that your cat will enjoy exploring for hours.

# African Safari Theme Park

"In the jungle, the mighty jungle, the lion sleeps ..."

Let kitty discover his inner lion as he stalks the wilds of this indoor jungle maze that you can set up in minutes anywhere in your home, and dismantle just as quickly.

## What You'll Need

- Potted plants and pots of kitty grass
- Cat toys and other intriguing items
- Large stuffed animals
- Catnip
- Cat treats

## How It Works

Before creating the kitty jungle, wait until your young lion is catnapping, dreaming of stalking marauding moles through his backyard savanna. Then choose a space that has enough room for you to set up your plants, grass, and hidden surprises. Basements are a good choice (since plants may tip over), but any room will do, as long as you're prepared for the possibility of sweeping up a little potting soil.

Begin with the jungle foliage: use thick, leafy houseplants and plants with long, waving grass (lemon grass, oat grass, and indoor cyprus plants work well and are inexpensive). Create a pathway, lined with plants, from one end of the room to the other. Place the plants fairly close together, but allow some room in between the pots, so your bold hunter can slip in and around the leaves and grass. Mix in some long cat grass (kitty will need green energy food for his safari adventure), and you've got your jungle! The more plants you add, the denser the forest and the more interesting the maze, but the number and types of plants you use is, of course, up to you.

CAUTION:  There are a large number of plants that are toxic to cats. Organizations like the Cat Fanciers' Association — www.cfa.org/articles/plants. html — offer much useful information on the subject. Find out which plants to avoid before investing too much time and money in your jungle.

Once you've created your grassy maze, it's time to add some surprises for your jungle cat. Hide toy mice and treats among the plants, along with cat-nip sacks, small plastic balls, and other kitty favorites. Tuck the toys and treats behind pots and under leaves. Cats have a great time wandering through the foliage, chewing on grass, and uncovering all the exciting things you've hidden.

Finally, add a couple of kitty-sized stuffed animals to give Leo Jr. a little faux competition. Stuffed tigers, lions, cheetahs, and chimps — craftily hiding behind large plants and grass — will keep kitty on his toes as he stalks through his indoor forest.

When everything's ready, it's time to wake kitty so he can begin his expedition. All his big cat dreams will be fulfilled as he explores his mighty indoor jungle. As he begins his safari, play a little background music for inspiration (don't all cats love Pete Seeger and the Tokens?), and kitty's off and hunting!

Wimoweh!

# Pussy's Playground

Okay, so your cat is a few years older now. Maybe he's a bit bored and cynical these days. He's knocked off his share of spiders and mice; he's tasted the forbidden 'nip. Maybe his catnaps have turned into full-blown snore-fests. Maybe he's asking himself, "Yawn. Is that all there is?"

It's time to shake Mr. Lazy out of the doldrums and let him relive the glories and giddy delights of his kittenhood. Time to get him back on the playground!

## What You'll Need

- A good-sized space with two furniture-free walls and an empty corner
- Ping-pong balls, paper, soft felt, and small plastic balls
- An assemblage of games and toys you've used before (described below)
- An executive mini-basketball hoop, used for paper ball games in the office
- A roll of painter's tape

## How It Works

The great thing about playgrounds is the variety of activities for kids to do and all the equipment available for them to play on, all concentrated in one place. Cats, of course, aren't kids, but like children, they do enjoy their diversions. They like to be entertained, and they like to try new things. When cats are in that certain mood, they can be considered to be, well, hyperactive.

But really, cats like girls (and boys) just wanna have fun. So, rather than forcing a daily dose of Kitalin down their little gullets, give them activities to do!

And Pussy's Playground is the place to do it.

First, mark out a few play areas on the floor with your painter's tape. This tape is easy to peel off, and it doesn't leave marks, so you'll be able to reclaim the area as a human space once puss has finished playing.

Tape off areas for a basketball court, a handball court, and, if you have the room, a little ice cube hockey arena. Use the corner space for your handball court — having a ricochet wall adds to the fun when you play this game and doubles the action.

Next, set up your Crazy Susan and Teeter-Totter Tumble. Every good playground has a merry-go-round and a seesaw, and now yours does, too.

Place kitty's Tunnel of Love (page 108) at one end of the space, and at the other end, kitty's ballfield. This area should include a chair for slugger to sit on to play Toss 'n' Swat and the other Batter Up! games he's learned to master.

Invite your cat into the tunnel, tempting him with a peacock feather or MouseStickle. When he emerges, he'll be ready to play some more, so keep him going with Crazy Susan, Teeter-Totter Tumble, and a rousing game of Smackdown!

Bounce a few ping-pong balls off the wall in the corner, and let kitty try to keep them in play. Chances are they'll fly out of bounds, but who cares? (You're not still trying to keep score, are you?) If your cat starts to lose interest, bring out the bowl of ice, and start flicking cubes across the floor for a rousing game of Ice Cube Hockey. Now how about a game of one-on-one? Toss paper and ping-pong balls at your mini-basketball hoop — pretend you're Michael Jordan while kitty plays defense, but just remember: no fair dunking!

You get the idea: with Pussy's Playground, you've arranged a great bunch of simple games, all in one place, and you're keeping your cat active, happy, and alert. And what cat wouldn't leap at the chance just to fool around and act like a crazy kitten again?

# THE GREAT (SAFE) OUTDOORS

Why do warm, secure, well-fed kitties constantly insist that they want to go outside? We, their devoted human slaves, provide them with good food, cozy beds, back rubs, foot rubs, belly rubs, and brushings. We set them up with kitty condos, kitty beds, kitty entertainment centers, and compatible kitty pals. Yet, they try to get outside, and if we — heaven forbid! — ever leave a door ajar, our cats will be out cruising the 'hood, half a mile away, faster than we can call 911.

Maybe romance is in the air. Maybe your little stud has been making connections behind your back (a little payback for that neutering visit to the vet) via Date-a-Tom.com. Hey, he can dream, can't he?

Blame it on instinct, boredom, or that deadly kitty trait — curiosity. Whatever the reason, your indoor cat will probably always be saddled with the inescapable urge to slip out of the confines of his safe, but somewhat predictable, indoor domestication.

How can we help kitties out of this fix? (Even if we've had them fixed?) Get 'em outside! It's easier than you'd think, and with a little patience, vigilance, and planning, you can provide a great safe outdoor experience for your cat and not have to worry about the inherent dangers that do many outdoor cats in — speeding cars, coyotes, dogs, and owls, to name just a few.

Yes, you can turn your inside cat out – and you can do it safely.

# Kitty Escapade with Harness and Leash

You might think your cat would never stand for this, but if you've got an indoor guy or gal who's itching to mingle with the birds and the trees, this activity is definitely worth a try.

We've been strolling outside with our cats for years — and once the kitties got past a brief initial adjustment period, our daily harness and leash escapades have been as easy as, well, a walk in the park.

## What You'll Need

- Thin nylon tethers to use as long leashes, available at most pet stores (the thin ones are usually sold for small dogs)
- A cat harness — also available at pet stores

## How It Works

(1) Introduce your cat to the harness. Be prepared: at first, your wary cat may not fully embrace your efforts. *No! Are you insane? You are not strapping that thing around ME, buddy!* So, begin the process slowly. Let kitty examine the harness on the floor: he'll sniff it, paw it, chew it a bit. These harnesses are made out of tough nylon straps; unless your cat's a Great White, chances are he won't do much damage.

When he's ready, gently slip one loop over his head. He'll shake it off, but try it again. Soon, he'll realize it's nothing to fear. At that point . . .

(2) Secure the harness around your kitty. There are two types of kitty harnesses you can buy: the double-loop style and the figure eight. The double-loop has two fasteners — one for a loop which goes around the neck, and one for a loop around the belly. The figure eight style is designed as one continuous piece with only one fastener. You adjust the size of the neck loop (the top of the figure eight) to fit over your cat's head. Then you secure the second loop (the bottom half of the eight) around kitty's back, fastening it under his stomach. Small plastic snaps (like the ones used on backpacks) lock the ends in place on both styles of harness.

At this point, kitty may freak out again (think bucking bronco in the OK Corral), but he'll get used to it pretty quickly. Praise him, and tell him how gorgeous he is wearing his new accoutrement. Oh, Tuffy! Aren't you handsome! Soon, if all goes well, he'll be strutting around the house, showing off his new outfit. Now it's time to . . .

(3) Attach the leash to the harness. When your cat's relaxed and standing still, casually sidle up to him and attach the tether to the little metal loop on the back of the harness. If you're careful and don't restrict his movement in any way, he won't even realize you've done it. Now let him roam around the house as you follow him, holding the tether up and away from his back. Just stay behind him, hold the lead — sort of like the queen's servant holding up the train of the royal gown. If you've been living with cats for a while, this is a role you're probably used to performing.

(4) Set some mini-boundaries.
Here's the skinny: you can't walk a cat. You can't make them heel or stay. Not really. However, they will stop when they run out of lead, and it is possible to redirect them. So practice this on your walks through the house. Every so often, as you're marching along on your kitty parade, stop and let your cat realize he can't go any farther. Let him run out of tether and pull against the lead. Just stand there, don't pull back or try to direct him.

At first he will loathe, despise, or at least, highly resent having this restriction placed upon him. But . . . he will get used to it. Try taking a step or two in a different direction, accompanied by the gentlest of tugs on the lead. He may get the idea he'd rather head off where you want to go — just don't try to force him. Gradually he'll get accustomed to the harness and leash and the idea of these gentle limits.

And when he does, you'll both be ready to . . .

(5) Head outside. This is an exciting time in the life of every cat and her human companion. Freedom, grass, and glory! Birds in the trees, sun in the sky, chipmunks and bugs to be eaten. As our cats tell us after returning from a good outdoor romp: *It doesn't get much better 'n this!* And you'll feel the same way, too, although you'll probably pass on the outdoor dining.

As with every step in this activity, you'll want to proceed through this one slowly. Never take your cat and simply carry her outside. Her first instinct will be to hide and run back inside the house. Instead, open the door and let her move at her own pace. Your job is to simply follow, holding the lead, and let her get her bearings. Caution and self-defense will be first on any cat's agenda, so give her all the space she needs — all you need is patience. If she wants to run back inside after a minute on the deck, fine — let her do it.

As kitty becomes used to the new environment, she'll want to go for longer walks. It's a good idea not to stray too far. Cats can easily become frightened by anything: trucks, odd noises, kids on bikes – anything they perceive as threats will send them running. So beware: the last thing you want is to be a half-mile from home with a frantic, panicky kitty.

Our cat walks are confined to our yard (which is fairly large) and short half-block strolls down the street. We can almost always get back inside the house quickly if the cats decide to hightail it and run. But we've been caught off-guard on a few occasions, with predictable results: tangled tethers, shredded arms, and hissing kitties.

Remember that cats count on their mobility as their first defense, and if they can't run and hide to protect themselves because they are on a leash, they'll be frightened and feel defenseless.

Finally, understand that you are not walking a poodle. I've yet to experience a "brisk walk" with my cats; they like to stop, stare, sit, and chew grass. Cat exercise usually involves some yoga stretches, followed by long moments of meditation. They are definitely not about jogging. So when you're outside with kitty and leash, try to become one with your feline. Enjoy the long contemplative moments in the cool fresh air. Let Mr. Puss stare at whatever he's decided to fixate on that day. You never know: you'll probably discover just how fascinating a twitching squirrel tail can be.

# Double Cat Fantasy

It's every cat person's dream: strolling triumphantly around the yard, led proudly by two high-steppin' kitties, their tails swishing expressively, straight up in the air.

Is it possible to walk two cats on a leash? At the same time? Read on, intrepid cat fantasist, you'll find out how to do it.

## What You'll Need

- Two or three nylon tethers
- Two cat harnesses
- Two leash-ready cats

## How It Works

First, clip your tethers together so that you've created one long leash. Most tethers are about 60 inches long — joining two or three together will give you ten or fifteen feet.

Next, assemble your cats. They should be prepped and well-practiced at the art of leading humans around on a leash. (This is not an activity for newbies; your cats should each have plenty of leash-strolling practice under their tails before you attempt walking two together.)

With your cats harnessed up and your long tether ready, you can begin your walk. Clip one end of the tether to one cat's harness and the other end to your second cat. Hold the tether in the middle and step outside.

Your delighted cats will charge ahead, but it's simple enough to keep control by allowing each one to explore, yet establishing the limits of the tether by holding on to the middle.

Your cats may want to walk together, or they may head off in different directions. This technique works either way. You'll be able to parade around the yard, both cats leading the way, or you can let each explore in his own direction. If the cats choose to go it alone, they'll set the limits themselves: the tether will let each go only so far; they'll stop where they are when that happens. When my cats go in opposite directions, I often drop the leash without fear they will run off. Each cat provides a natural anchor for the other — I can sit back on the porch step and watch them explore.

Again a caution about things that may scare your cats: you definitely don't want to be caught unaware when one or both of your cats become frightened. So stay alert. If both kitties panic at the same time when they are tethered together, you'll have to intervene quickly — ignoring claws, teeth, and tangled tethers — guaranteeing a kitty-human bonding experience you won't soon forget.

# Stakeout

Calling all cats! Calling all cats! Be on the lookout for three annoying chipmunks and a squirrel stealing nuts! Last seen in the vicinity of Elm Tree and Tulip Bed ...

## What You'll Need

- Several long nylon tethers
- One or two sturdy metal corkscrew stakes (usually used for backyard dogs)
- Your intrepid police cadet kitties

## How It Works

That inevitable day has finally arrived, the day you've longed for, yet dreaded. Kitty wants to head out on yard patrol on his own without Mom or Dad tagging along behind him.

How do you give him his independence (without giving up the keys to the car)?

Stakeout is the win-win solution for both the independent-minded kitty (aren't they all?) and his apprehensive bipeds. Just as he was able to adapt to harness and leash, your cat will quickly catch on to tether and stake and learn to enjoy this activity's freedom — and its limits.

Preparation is the same as the with the harness and leash activities — which, hopefully, have been rousing successes. Now that your outdoor guy or gal is used to strolling while wearing a harness and tether, he or she will be able to hang out in the yard alone — this time, though, you'll attach the tether to a stake in the ground or to a deck or porch railing.

Start him off slowly, always keeping an eye on him, making sure he doesn't try to wiggle out of his harness. He'll realize you're not walking with him and then understand he can go only so far. The tether, attached to the stake, will keep him safely near your house while giving him the sense of freedom all Indy cats desire.

Always keep an eye on your cat. It may be too easy to forget he's out there, so keep watch, frequently, through the window. As noted in the cautions previously mentioned, lots of things we take for granted are frightening to kitties.

(Our Maine coon, Forrest, has apparently decided that large, rattling delivery trucks are actually fire-breathing demons from Hell. And he'll run like hell anytime he hears one coming. When he's tethered outside, we always make sure that he has a clear path of escape to the door, in case one of these rolling fiends suddenly roars up the block.)

As kitties grow accustomed to this stakeout routine, you can add lengths of tether, giving them more room to roam. They'll enjoy poking around the yard on their own as long as they can quickly get back inside — so never stake them too far away from your door. Cats need to know how to find the nearest safe haven.

Finally, try another fun bonding activity: if you're working in the yard, move the stake, and let kitty patrol for squirrels and birds next to the spot where you're working. You'll both enjoy the company, while engaging in your own separate activities. Plus, you never know — your cat may want to take a break from his squirrel stakeout and decide to help you do a little digging.

PART THREE:

# Projects to Assemble

Many of us fantasize about being able to work with our cats as we build useful, satisfying projects. We imagine ourselves out in the garage or downstairs in our little basement shops, sawing wood, drilling holes, and hammering together impressive, creative structures. We like the idea that our cats would be learning a skill from us, one they could use all their lives and pass on to their kittens.

We'd teach young cats the basics, letting them merely observe human Mom or Dad measuring and fitting; then as they got a year or two older, we'd let them sit on the blueprints or fetch us the Phillips screwdriver or the Gorilla Glue, if the picture on the bottle didn't scare them. Finally, of course, they'd be building projects themselves (perhaps a custom-designed litter box), scoring wood with their little claws and brushing sawdust off the vise with their tails.

As appealing as these fantasies may be, the reality is that your cat has no interest in helping you build anything, even a better mousetrap. That's because your cat believes he is the better mousetrap and he has no desire to be replaced. Furthermore, if you've ever asked a cat to help you do anything, you already know that a cat's genetically coded predetermined response is to cast a withering look your way, which in effect says, *What are you, crazy?*

A cat's main goal when helping you work is to wait until you've reached a critical moment, when everything has to remain exactly in its place, and then stroll across the materials you're working on and demand to get his head rubbed.

So, fortunately, it is beyond the scope of this book and the abilities of its author to offer detailed instructions on how to build anything complex. This section does, however, include project ideas, resources for finding supplies, instructions, and kits, as well as descriptions of a few very simple projects you really can build at home, with or without the invaluable assistance of your kitty.

# Stairway to the Stars

Your kitty's already the star of your home, but, ambitious tree climber that he is, chances are he'll want to achieve even greater heights in his promising cat career as he scales the feline ladder of success. So why not give him a leg up?

The following 'stairway' is easy to build, interesting to look at, and fun and challenging for your little go-getter who's determined to claw his way to the top!

## What You'll Need

- Five 12 to 16 inches long  x 10 inch wide  x ½ inch pieces of wood
- One 14 inch long x  14 inch deep  by ½ inch deep piece of wood
- Twelve shelf brackets (different wall materials require different types of brackets, see below for additional information)
- Wood screws, anchor bolts, double stick tape or adhesive
- Six pieces of low-pile carpet or rubber (stair treads will work)
- A drill

## How to Build It

Assuming your cat doesn't weigh more than 20 pounds, a combination of anchor bolts  and L-shaped angle brackets may work best for securing the shelves to the wall. Depending on how much wall space you have for this project, use shelf boards that are between 12 and 16 inches long. Standard studs are generally 16 inches apart but this can vary. Anchor bolts are a good method if you choose the shorter length shelf in cases where the studs might not be where you need them.

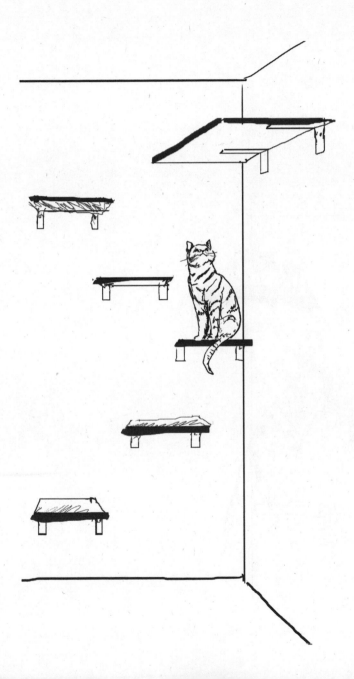

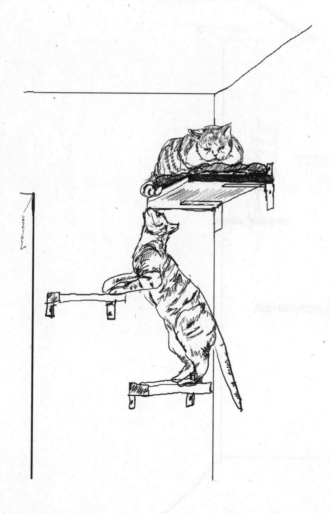

Mark on the wall where you will secure the shelf boards. Stagger the position of the shelves (see illustration) so your cats will be able to position themselves properly to make the leap from one shelf to the other.

Secure the L-shaped brackets to the underside of each shelf and inset from the edges. If you plan to use carpet pieces or rubber for the top (highly recommended to keep splinters at a minimum and make the tops safer footing for kitty) cut and affix the pieces to the top of each board. If you use rubber stair treads or something similiar, double stick tape will work or use rug glue for the carpet.

Attach the shelves to the wall.

## How It Works

Once you've constructed your stairway to the stars, let kitty discover it for himself. He'll already be curious, having watched you build it, so he'll be eager to try it out. He'll probably jump right up on the first shelf and easily begin climbing. Cats like to get up high where they feel safe, secure, and superior, so this stairway will make perfect sense to your kitty.

However, if your cat needs a little encouragement, pat the lowest shelf with your hand, or put a treat or catnip sack on it. If he makes it on to the first shelf, another treat will tempt him up to the second. Eventually he'll make his way to the top, but let him take his time. Never frighten him or catch him off-guard by simply picking him up and placing him high up on the top shelf. His first instinct might be to run, and he could leap down and hurt himself.

Once kitty's made it to the top on his own, he'll feel secure knowing he can climb up and down independently, and he'll be able to relax on high and enjoy the view. The stairway is the next best thing to having a tree growing inside your home, which, although unique, is an indoor design feature most homeowners tend to decline.

# The Leaning Tower of Kitties

If you build it, they will climb.

They can't help themselves. Cats have to climb on things, get up high, and look out at the world. So, if you can't grow a tree inside your home, you might want to consider installing a tower for your kitties.

If you know how to build one of these structures, you can create your own for a modest amount of money. They are all basically the same, no matter the make or style: wooden poles and perches, covered in carpeting material, and attached to a wide, sturdy base.

You can also buy these cat towers in almost any pet store. From the simple one-perch setup to the soaring multiperch skyscrapers that several kitties can enjoy at the same time, there is much to choose from when exploring the world of commercial kitty towers and condos.

The good ones, though, aren't cheap. Strong, sturdy, well-made towers are available, but they come at a price which may seem extravagant for wooden poles covered in carpet. However, if you opt for a flimsier model, you may find your cats swaying and dangling from their padded perch, and your kitty tower may start to resemble its famous counterpart in Pisa.

There are, of course, alternatives to the high-priced models. Search the Web and you'll probably find just the right item for you and your cash-conscious kitty.

The following e-tailers feature a vast array of kitty towers, condos, and structures:

www.cozycatfurniture.com/catgyms_cattowers.html
www.kittykondo.com/
www.petsmart.com

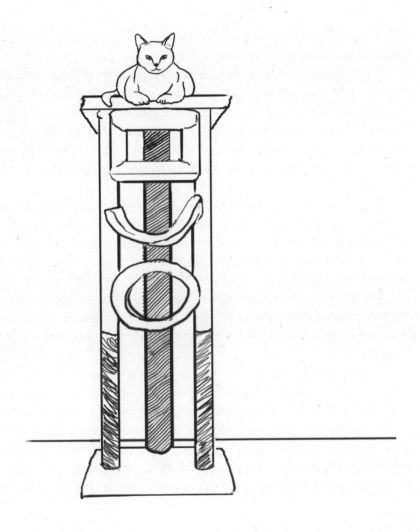

# Outdoor Enclosures

Please note the word choice in the title. The word *cages* is kittically incorrect, and you won't find it in this book.

That said, outdoor enclosures are basically, well, the "c" word, albeit really big ones that your cat can roam around in while enjoying the great outdoors. You can let your cats outside, but they'll really be inside, and they will be protected from cars, predators, and tough neighborhood bully cats who roam around looking for trouble. Inside a big enclosure, your cat can eat, sleep, play, whittle, and generally watch the world go by, safely protected behind the wire or mesh fencing.

Can you build one? Absolutely, if you know how to use basic tools and materials and can follow a design for the structure. However, there are an abundance of preassembled enclosures available to buy, as well as enclosure kits ready to assemble. With so many great enclosures on the market, it may be worth your time to see what's for sale in pet stores and on the Web.

The Web sites listed on the next page offer some excellent designs and intriguing shapes. These are only a sample of what's available, but if you are interested, investigate and see what suits you and your kitty's needs and budget.

Finally, I propose more dynamic, interactive experiences between humans and their companion cats. Simply opening the door and letting your kitties out into an enclosure may allow them to enjoy the fresh air and a taste of freedom safely, but it won't provide the same human/cat communicative experience you'll get walking them, watching them explore on their tethers, playing with them, and discovering the many facets of their complex and fascinating minds and personalities. Cats will reveal their true personalities once they understand that you are more than just the food provider and resident head scratcher. Sure, they'll take that — it's not a bad deal, but if you are willing to explore possibilities, you'll discover just how cool your cat friends really are.

WEB SOURCES FOR KITTY ENCLOSURES:

www.thepamperedpetmart.com — features the "Kittywalk," a long mesh tube for outdoor fun, sort of like a kitty metro
www.pawshop.com/koucatsy.html — includes a variety of interesting outdoor environments
www.TheCatsDen.net — sells elaborate, well-constructed enclosures and enclosure kits
www.just4cats.com — visit this site for do-it-yourself enclosures

EVEN MORE RESOURCES:

www.catmax.com.au
www.classypetshop.com
www.cats.about.com

# Tunnel of Love

What's better than an empty cardboard box just waiting for a kitty? How about several boxes, all lined up and taped together, filled with toys and treats?

Curious cats have to explore, and this easy-to-create kitty hideaway provides cats with a world of discovery. Of course, you can buy premade crinkle tunnels or similar toys for cats to jump into or crawl through, but why spend the money when you can easily make one yourself, using a few inexpensive, household items?

So start saving those cardboard delivery boxes you were going to recycle anyway, and put them to even better use. The Tunnel of Love awaits your adventurous cat!

And, yes, your kitty will love it.

## What You'll Need

- Several sturdy cardboard boxes, large enough for cats to stroll through
- A few rolls of nontoxic tape (Beware: some cats like to gnaw and eat this stuff)
- A box cutter or exacto knife
- Ribbons and string
- Assorted kitty toys and tempting treats

## How to Build It

Prepare your boxes by opening both ends and taping the flaps together, so you are creating a long, hollow square or rectangle from each box. If one end of the box is sealed and solid, simply cut away that section with your knife to open that end.

Once you have several boxes taped and ready, cut four or five square windows in selected boxes for kitty to look through and pop out of as she pleases. Create windows on the tops and sides of your boxes. Use various shapes — ovals, squares, rectangles — to keep these openings interesting little surprises for your cat.

Now you're ready to assemble your Tunnel of Love.

Begin by taping the boxes together, creating a strong connection by layering tape at the seam where the two boxes are joined. You can tape the boxes in a straight line, or angle them, using the flaps to create a bend, which will allow you to snake your tunnel back and forth in a zigzag pattern. Some cats will enjoy the zigzag challenge, others will balk if they don't see a straight passageway — experiment and find out what works for your kitties.

As you join the boxes together, tape some dangling strings and ribbons to the seam area, allowing the strings and ribbons to dangle inside the tunnel. You can add more of these throughout by taping some outside the cutout window sections you've already made and having the string hang through the opening. Tie a few toys to the strings and ribbons, which your cat will discover as she makes her way through the tunnel.

Once your tunnel is assembled, it's time for your cat to play.

## How It Works

Introduce kitty to the tunnel, and let her sniff around and explore it. She may want to dive right in, or she may be a trifle cautious. Let her take her time. She'll probably, find her way inside the tunnel eventually, but you can also encourage her by tossing a toy or treat inside or wiggling one of the ribbons, toys, or peacock feathers, which you've taped onto the cutout.

Once your cat is inside, keep the toys moving, jiggling the strings and ribbons and toys, enticing her farther into the tunnel. She'll also discover the cutouts and want to pop her head in and out. This is a good chance to use your peacock feather again. Wiggle it inside the tunnel from either opening at the ends, or use the cutouts for the same tantalizing purpose. You can also try running your fingers and nails across the surfaces of the box. (Fingernails sound a lot like little mice feet — so keep them moving.)

Some cats stay in these tunnels for hours — they're good hideouts — while other cats like to run in and out, thrilled with the adventure. Set it up in a spot where she normally strolls when she makes her daily rounds through the house.

Your kitty won't mind the morning commute to her food dish anymore, now that her route includes an exciting trip through the delightful Tunnel of Love. Beep! Beep!

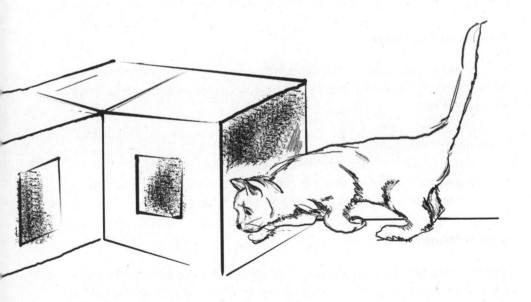

# Crinkle, Crinkle, Little Cat

Don't worry, you won't be wondering where he's at when he is inside the Crinkle Tunnel. You'll be able to hear his every move as he stretches, yawns, rolls, and swats at toys inside this ready-made, inviting tube that cats find as irresistible as plastic bubble wrap is to us bubble-popping humans.

## What You'll Need

- Crinkle tunnels! One or more (the more, the crinklier). They may be used alone or tied together to form a long, intriguing tube.
- A selection of toys and peacock feathers to drive your kitty wild

## Where to Purchase

Most large pet stores sell Crinkle Tunnels; however, you may find the best variety on the Web. Check out the following e-sources for inventive variations on this popular item:

- www.kittykondo.com
- www.petco.com — (this site features a long 59-inch tunnel)
- www.grandinroad.com — (this site offers tunnels which can be tied together)
- buy several and create a supertunnel for your adventurous cat

## How It Works

There's no mystery here: cats enjoy a safe, enclosed space where they can hide out, peer out, and occasionally pop out at all the interesting objects that happen to move past them. Other cats, spiders, dust balls, bare feet, ankles, and the unfortunate, wayward mouse are all fair game when kitty's in a mood and hiding out in a good location.

Providing your cat with a good crinkle tunnel gives him added pleasure because he'll not only have a place to lurk, but he'll also enjoy the exquisite auditory satisfaction of creating a whole new annoying sound, which he can add to his repertoire of scratching, hissing, and demanding meows — infuriating noises that drive humans to distraction on a regular basis.

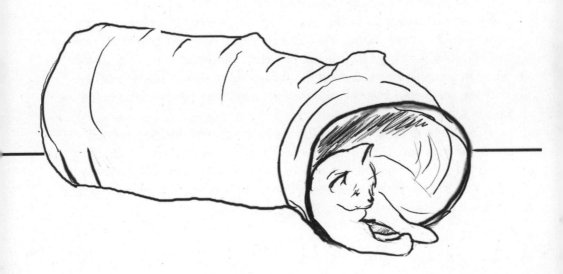

To get started, set up your crinkle tunnel in a convenient place. You don't want it in the middle of a high foot-traffic area (like a hallway or a kitchen), but you do want to position it in an area where your stealth cat can hide out and pounce on things when the need arises.

Once you introduce him to the tunnel, he'll probably take to it right away. A test paw inside the opening will create the sound he can't resist — *Oh, baby! There's some sweet crinkling going on in here!* — and soon he'll be scooting inside the tube wiggling with anticipation, certain that no one knows he's there. *Heh, heh. Wait'll Miss Precious sashays her fluffy little tail past this bad boy — it ain't gonna be pretty.*

Of course, most cats don't seem to make the connection between the alluring crinkle sound and the fact that this noise they love also alerts all comers to the possibility of the kitty ambush. More puzzling, yet quite common, is the, shall we say "big-boned" cat who can't quite fit his entire bulky self, particularly (as in the case of our cat, Forrest) his enormous posterior, into the crinkle tunnel. Who does he think he's kidding with his rear half and long, flicking tail sticking out one end? However, as they say, "Denial ain't just a river in Egypt," and cats — big-boned or not — seem to believe they are completely invisible once they get even their heads tucked inside the crinkle tunnel.

Try not to disillusion your big-boned kitty. Act terrified and surprised when he pops out at you — feign a heart attack if you have to — anything to avoid letting him know you knew he was lying in wait (and spilling halfway out of the crinkle tunnel). As in all interactions with your cat, it is most important to do all you can to protect kitty's fragile self-image.

## Tunnel Toy Variation

When kitty's not in an ambushin' mood, you and he can still enjoy the crinkle tunnel if you introduce a few good toys.

Try flinging some stuffed mice into the tunnel and see if your cat chases after them. Once he's inside, he'll be waiting for more, so roll more items his way and let him try to catch them. Surprise him with a sneak attack of your own, and toss a mouse or two inside from the rear just to keep him hopping. With your fingernails, imitate scratchy mouse feet scurrying along on the outside of the tunnel,

Wiggle a peacock feather inside the tube to entice him and get his attention. Once he's inside the tunnel, use the feather again, brushing it against the openings where his head and tail are or wiggling it outside (imitating prey) to get him up and running. Use your plastic wand to dangle feathers outside the tunnel's opening to create a fluttering diversion.

There are many possibilities for combination games once your cat's inside the tunnel. Revisit the Techno Games section of this book and watch what happens when Laser Sprite pays a visit to dance and flit outside the crinkle tunnel!

# The Mr. Kitty Portable Self-Grooming Device

Most cats count on their humans to be their personal valets/slaves, a role which we are usually delighted to perform seven days a week, at all hours of the day and the evening. But what happens if the humans are not around? Occasionally we do need to leave the house to go to work so we can earn a little cash to buy fabulous food and terrific toys for our furry masters.

Cats can get cranky when they want food, recreation, or even a good

brushing. A healthy supply of cat chow and toys left out when humans are not around can solve the first two problems, but how do you satisfy your fastidious cat's perfectly natural desire to be well-groomed, brushed, and pampered?

The Mr. Kitty Portable Self-Grooming Device is the answer.

## What You'll Need

- One flexible nylon brush, about 24 to 30 inches long (a refrigerator brush used for cleaning the coils works well)
- A solid flat piece of square-shaped wood; 24 inches and about ½ inch thick
- A piece of carpet remnant large enough to cover the wood and wrap over the edges
- Double-sided carpet tape or glue
- A pair of wire snips, a drill, staple gun, and possibly a hammer

## How To Build It

You'll be constructing a simple arc using the flexible nylon brush, which is made with twisted wire. Refrigerator brushes come with a plastic handle; use the snips or a wire cutter to clip off the handle so only the brush remains. Bend the brush into a U shape and mark where you'll be drilling the holes.

Drill two holes through the wood. The diameter of the holes (and the size of your drill bit) depends on the thickness of the wire; however make the holes a bit smaller so the brush ends fit snugly into each hole.

Using the carpet tape, glue, or staples attach the carpet to the board, be sure to wrap the carpet around the edges to the underside. Turn the board over and poke through the carpet to mark where to insert the brush.

Bend the bristle wire into the U shape again and insert into the holes through to the other side. Often, the tension from the flexible brush is enough to hold the brush in place. If not, flip the base over and untwist enough of the wire on the bottom using a pair of pliers. Flatten each piece against the bottom of the board — this will hold the brush in place. Either way, be sure to use a piece of tape or furniture protector pads (used for chair and table legs) to protect your floors.

Now flip the base over and you'll have a little kitty car wash, sans the H2O!

Time to try it on your kitty.

## How It Works

Once your cat figures this one out, she'll happily wiggle through the arc, giving herself a nice relaxing back and side scratch, while shedding a bunch of would-be hairball buildup.

Your cat may not take to the Mr. Kitty Portable Grooming Device at first, so you'll have to show her the ropes. Chances are, you won't be able to wiggle through it yourself, but you can show her with your hand and arm and perhaps pull her favorite stuffed toy through it a few times to give her the idea.

Place your cat next to the arc, and let her brush up against it and rub her chin along the bristles. This thing actually feels good to cats, and they can control the pace and pressure of the self-brushing (unlike the occasional torture sessions we put them through trying to untangle the massive knots and hairy clumps encountered during our often aborted grooming sessions). Instead of the wild hissing and flashing claw defense kitty may use to fend off the dreaded brush, now kitty will be in charge. And with cats, that's how it should be.

Soon, your cat will be rubbing against the arc, slipping through it, and purring contentedly as she becomes accustomed to this relaxing pleasure device. In fact, she may grow to like The Mr. Kitty Portable Grooming Device so much, that you may begin to feel left out:

"Doesn't kitty want me to brush her anymore?"

Don't despair, and try not to send your kitty on a guilt trip. Getting her human strokes will always be first on her list, but a little variety never hurts and — as is important in any relationship — may even keep that kitty-human bond interesting and exciting.

PART FOUR:
# Chillin' Out

At this point, your cat has done it all. She's swatted dangling strings, chased chubby mice, defeated teddy bears and annoying clowns, scored ice cube goals, ping-pong points, and triumphed in Volleyball Smackdown. Kitty's been a good sport, playing all sorts of rigorous games on Pussy's Playground, and she's trekked deep into a faux African jungle. She's worked out, spaced out, been walked outside and staked out, and she's even learned to work on your computer.

So what's next?

Maybe now it's time to kick back a bit and let kitty indulge in her (or his) favorite pastime, namely a dreamy afternoon snooze. Cats, we are told, sleep anywhere between 18 and 22 hours a day, and they don't need to take a pill to do it. Cats instinctively understand the importance of sleep. They need to store up their energy for the evening hunt or, in the case of indoor cats, the evening stroll to the food bowl.

Chill out time, for cats or humans, is usually a solitary pursuit. So how can we stay involved with our kitties while they're sacking out? Easy — just chill out with them.

The following activity requires little more from you than the ability to recline in a prone position and to indulge kitty her simple pleasures.

# Kitty Kneads Me

She kneads me! She really kneads me!

No, you're not accepting a best actor award; you're just lying on the couch, letting kitty walk all over you — a situation with which, by now, you should be all too familiar.

## What You'll Knead

- A comfortable sofa
- A cat with claws
- An ability to endure acupuncture-like discomfort

## How It Works

Lie on the couch on a lazy afternoon or during any of kitty's traditional naptimes. Let your cat know you'll be taking a nap, too, by yawning loudly and emitting other verbal signals that will tell kitty you're ready for a relaxing siesta. Remain on the couch, yawn a few more times and begin to fall asleep. Your cat will sense if you're getting too comfortable and will move quickly to intervene.

As kitty approaches, pat your belly and let your cat know she's welcome to hop up and share the couch with you. She probably won't need an invitation. Like most cats, she can't resist the prospect of conking out on a warm human gut, especially if it's a soft one. And she'll be delighted that, once again, you've chosen to lie on the sofa instead of punishing yourself in the gym with a torturous abdominal workout.

Once kitty is aboard, standing on your spongy belly, she will begin to knead. She will work her claws like a little baker preparing flabby loaves of bread. Try not to focus on the pain; instead, be happy that you are providing your beloved cat with so much well deserved pleasure. As the kneading becomes more intense, don't be alarmed by the distant, obsessed, vaguely psychotic look on kitty's face. She'll be back to her usual demanding self as soon as kneading time is over.

If, at any time during this procedure, kitty's sharp needle-claws become unbearable, employ time-tested martial arts' techniques, used for centuries by ancient masters to help them endure horrible pain. Picture yourself elsewhere. Imagine yourself back in the neighborhood tattoo parlor, and remember all the fun you had there.

Once kitty's had her way with you, she will abruptly stop kneading, sigh, collapse on your chest, and immediately begin snoring. Now is the time to bond with your sweet, sleeping cat. Take this opportunity to catch forty winks yourself. When kitty wakes up again, you'll need them.

# Cats-on-tumtum-asana

Cats are natural yogis. You knew that, or if you didn't, you do now; but either way, you've probably marveled at your kitty's flexibility and graceful strength as she completes her various stretching routines throughout the day. Many yoga postures are named for animals and animal movements, and several are named for cats. (The Cat Stretch and the Lion Pose, for example.)

Occasionally you may have been inspired to try some of these feline-inspired poses yourself, and, perhaps have discovered to your dismay that we all can't be as flexible as cats.

Take heart. Even if your rusty joints prevent you from participating fully in kitty's yoga class, there is a rewarding pose all humans and cats can enjoy together.

## What You'll Need

- A floor with a carpet (or, alternatively, use a sofa or a bed).
- Your feline yogi or yogini

## How It Works

Ideally, this pose should be practiced immediately following kneading activity. Kitty will already be on your stomach, in a semi-trance and, following a day of vigorous activity, be ready to practice Cats-on-tumtum-asana, also known as Kitty Rest.

Remain on the floor or sofa in prone position with your cat resting on your stomach. Begin to gently massage his head and shoulders with your fingertips. As kitty's purr deepens, coordinate your breathing with his, allowing your breath to gradually slow. If you are so inclined, begin to purr yourself as you generate a soft vibrating breath from the back of your throat.

Once you and kitty are in full purr-mode, appreciate yoga kitty's warm, furry body resting serenely on your chest. With your eyes half-closed, allow yourself to transcend into kitty consciousness. Admire kitty's fuzzy chin resting on his paws, a Buddha-like half-smile creasing his perfect little face.

Drift into deep relaxation and experience Nirvana with your cat.

Ahhh. There's no other place you'd rather be, and what could be better than that?